I0461978

Nature in the Internet Age

Nature in the Internet Age

C·Me

C·Me

2017

Copyright © 2017 by C·Me

All rights reserved. This book or any portion thereof may not be reproduced or used in any manner whatsoever without the express written permission of the publisher except for the use of brief quotations in a book review or scholarly journal.

First Printing: 2017

ISBN 978-0-244-62328-9

C·Me
www.c-me.global

U.S. trade bookstores and wholesalers: Please contact editor@c-me.global
.

Contents

I. THE PRIZE FIGHT

It's self-evident that the internet and related information and communication technologies have transformed the world. Still, the quality and force of the shift have not been fully appreciated.

The transformation was a one-two punch, resulting in technical knockout. The jab stopped a trend to increasing social entropy that characterized the pre-internet era. Society was fragmented and the pieces were drifting apart; now, though still fragmented, its bits are corralled by technology. The cross that followed shattered the physical unity of the world, that old, a priori conviction of nature's unity that was the basis of what is still, anachronistically, known as Natural History. It caused a kind of symmetry between the physical and subjective realms: both made of dissimilar bits, held in check in a kind of simulated continuity. The resulting state was a positive culture of generalized, controlled fragmentation.

We didn't see the second punch coming, feel it hit us, or sense the fracturing it caused. This is because there is no 'we,' just a large number of individual cusses, half-pulled and pushed into new, technology-enabled relations with others. The technology has introduced ambiguities: what is and is not a person, the extent to which a person's subjective, inner uniqueness is an artefact, and how bodies in the old sense of flesh-and-blood people fit in. This ambiguity effectively overturned the mind-body dualism of the pre-internet era, allowing its mental cacophony to spread into bodies. The new technology has been a boon to those members of society pre-disposed to see the world as fragmented, who take comfort and power from clutching, quite literally, their social interfaces in the palms of their hand, outsourcing gestalt and direction to cyberspace. The paradox of simultaneous control and surrender that the internet offers has been compared to surfing, an association so engrained that it is no longer even a metaphor.

This initial essay, first of the quartet comprising this book, amounts to holding ammonia under the nose of the groggy: *where am I?* The second reveals that our post-TKO world is not unprecedented. Other societies, though technically impoverished in comparison, have been similarly fragmented. We can see their traits in ours, expressed, for us, as a function of the adaptation of our social organization to the capabilities and imperatives of the internet and related technologies. The third essay shows the internet zeitgeist colonizing physics, the crowning science of the pre-millennial world of unitary nature. Physics has largely completed a procedural, generational, and theoretical realignment to the fissured realities of our times. My last essay examines the role of a ubiquitous class of artefacts in the new era—the lowly, high-tech PowerPoint presentation—in purposeful collective action. Presentation-events, real and virtual, are the stuff of which organizational cohesion and action now are made. Their logic and rhetoric are at odds with prior ways of assimilating and deciding, but attuned to the fragmented world that we are and are in.

The Jab

The modern era was a rising tide of alienation. A century ago even the most developed countries of the Western world were still mainly rural and agrarian. People tended farms and worked in fields, and were pretty much outdoors all day. They worried about things like rainfall and insects as direct threats to their livelihood and even survival. They might have recently gotten electricity, but even if they did the technology of daily life was still pretty simple.

Nowadays, of course, only a small rump of people still farm and their numbers would be fewer but for subsidies. Most people live in cities. Almost everyone, rural and urban alike, is insulated from nature, living in technology in ways that were formerly unimaginable, with air conditioning, electricity, plumbing, appliances, entertainment, cars, communications, and so on. It is a struggle to get kids outside to play anymore, even in the attenuated green areas of modern cities and suburbs. Most prefer to be inside on their computers, tablets or smartphones. Such farms as do remain are agribusinesses, and, to the extent that they are labour-intensive, rely on seasonal labour.

The move to cities and factories has ever been associated with the destruction of old solidarities. By the middle of the nineteenth century, radicals like Marx were focused on the alienation of the masses and predicted a revolution that would restore wholeness. Within the mainstream, the academic discipline of sociology emerged around Tönnies' distinction between mechanical and organic solidarity, the former being simple communities made up of similar people who knew each other, the latter complex societies assembled from disparate people who did not. Coeval with sociology was psychology, focused on helping people deal with the neuroses of modern life. Waves of immigration occurred, and even if the immigrants stayed in enclaves that largely recreated conditions back home, their descendants assimilated and by the third generation were absorbed within the mainstream culture, creating intergenerational gaps and dissonances that were new.

There have been plateaus and sometimes major ups and downs, but the general trend has been toward higher individual income. In consequence people buy and own many more things than they used to. Ownership of sometimes massive amounts of stuff does not just alter people's relationship to nature and others; it also alters people's relationship to things in general.

The simplest way to think about our changing, more estranged relation to things is in terms of what is often referred to as the cash nexus (the term, again, originates with Marx). Broadly, everything now has a price and can be bought and sold for money, which once stood for precious metal but now exists by government fiat and popular acceptance. This means that we think of things in terms of an abstract exchange value rather than intrinsic worth or a close weighing of disparate features for barter.

The economy is built on the division of labour, trade and innovation. As a result of this powerful combination we no longer make much of what we have and consume; somebody else made it. Nowadays, probably a bunch of other people made it. They mostly don't know each other and are scattered around the world.

Our rising incomes have enabled us to accumulate lots of things, presenting dilemmas that our forebears, in more minimalist times, did not have to face. We have to think about where to put it all, what to throw away, and what to replace, and have special conceptual categories for stuff we don't want but hang on to anyhow, stuff we don't want and don't want to hang onto but are not ready to get rid of just yet, and stuff we do want and will hang on to but aren't going to use for the foreseeable future. Hoarding is a recognized psychological disorder.

This is quite apart from the stores of money that we have in banks or other investments, that may in some convoluted way be used by others to buy their stuff, or to buy stuff notionally on our behalf, but also represent our diffuse and fungible rights to buy more tangible stuff on our own at some point in the future.

Finally, what we buy will at some basic, recyclable level be made from natural materials, but it is essentially an artefact fashioned by humans, for the express purpose of selling it to people like us. This raises the question of who really controls the stuff we have and how we use it. There is a grey area between consumer choice and producer decision, between marketing to autonomous and empowered agents and manipulating feckless buyers.

It is clear that as people have had more money to spend, they have generally chosen to spend it in ways that give them more autonomy and separation from others, whether such spending relates to their development through education and other goods that increase prospects or to life in the present. Such preferences in turn are part of the reason they have more money to spend, economic growth being linked to both consumer spending and investment in education. Preferences for autonomy and separation are less cited as drivers of economic growth, but it is difficult to think of geographic, sectorial and inter-firm labour flows or urbanization and specialization without them. The overall preferential tendency for autonomy and separation has been labelled individualism. It has been celebrated, e.g., a romanticizing of "rugged individualism" as a distinctive American trait and font of achievement. It has also been criticized as a character defect, particularly when Western economic growth and social dysfunction are compared to more "collectivist" Asian societies. As Geert Hofstede showed in *Culture's Consequences,* though, when variations in individualism across the world are normalized for differences in income per capita, more than 80% of the difference between countries disappears, and the partisans and critics turn out to be fighting over the scraps that are left.

Francis Fukuyama summed up the sorry state of organic solidarity across the developed world in his 1999 book, *The Great Disruption, Human Nature and the Reconstitution of Social Order.* He looked at a broad set of developed countries around the world, including Japan and Korea to ward off Western bias, and saw that "social capital" declined across the board, in a persistent and significant way, starting in the 1960s. Social capital, like organic solidarity and individualism, is of course a construct, with its own history stretching back to 1916, popularized in recent decades by the sociologist James Coleman and political scientist Robert Putnam. By adopting it Fukuyama meant to highlight that community solidarity is a valuable asset, built up over time through the exercise of private virtues. Conversely it can be spent, dissipated and lost, gradually or quickly.

To avoid being just an erudite jeremiad, Fukuyama needed concrete evidence. By definition there can be none for a construct directly; even if it were possible in principle to get some, the odds of being able to find good, hard data for it consistently across decades for a broad set of countries are vanishingly small. So he instead relied on indirect data to measure social capital. Specifically, he looked at crime, surveys of social trust, and statistics on divorce and out-of-wedlock births. They all backed his thesis. The notional value of social capital can be operationalized as the cost of crime, including consequences of the act itself as well as efforts, private and public, at prevention, remediation and justice; lower trust, including more lawyers, thicker contracts, and more time spent on formal and informal due diligence; and dealing with children reared in poor and broken homes without adequate attention, role models, stability, financial security, and love, as children and later on as dysfunctional adults.

The other way to back up his point is by identifying what specifically caused everything to go south, more or less in lockstep worldwide, starting in the early 1960s. The trigger, in his view, was oral contraception, which hit the market in the US in 1960 and spread quickly, notwithstanding controversy, to the near-ubiquitous availability it now enjoys. There are many good things about liberating sex from procreation, giving women greater control over their reproductive lives, and helping them get massively out of the home and into the workplace. But it certainly has proved devastating over time to the traditional family, as the potent social pressures that used to be brought to bear on couples to marry when the women got pregnant, and men to provide physical and financial support through thick and thin, were undermined.

From his vantage point on the cusp of the new millennium, Fukuyama frankly didn't see much ground for optimism. So he reaches back into the primordial prehistory of mankind, and even beyond to primatology, to argue that humans have always been a bunch of little social capitalists. The urge to build community solidarity runs so deep and strong that some way out of the impasse and decline will no doubt be found.

Since he wrote *The Great Disruption*, measurable social capital has evolved in interesting ways, suggesting a certain fracturing of his concept. Violent crime has seen a stunning decline. Murder has dropped strongly in every one of the 15 countries he analysed over the past few decades. According to OECD statistics, the simple average murder rate for the set of countries dropped from 2.1 to 1.1 per hundred thousand, or by 47%. Divorce rates are also down, slightly, with the simple average across the countries dropping from 2.16 to 2.13 per thousand people or 1%. The general tendency to decline is masked by a sharp increase in the divorce rate in Spain, which was extremely low at the turn of the millennium and now has largely caught up. Excluding Spain the simple average divorce rate dropped from 2.24 to 2.12 or by 5%, with 11 countries showing declines. The incidence of births out of wedlock, on the other hand, has soared. Just over a quarter of all children were illegitimate when Fukuyama wrote; now over a third (37%) is. Indeed, the word "illegitimate" scarcely applies to such a mainstream phenomenon.

Measures of trust, as Fukuyama pointed out, are the trickiest to measure. Trust in what? Gallup provides a time series for the US detailed across 15 separate institutions. The big winner since Fukuyama's book has been small business, which has seen a 10% increase in the number of people who responded that they trusted it a "great deal" or "quite a lot," and 3% decline in whose who said they trusted it very little or not at all. The criminal justice system and the military also saw modest improvements in reported levels of trust. On the other hand, the dominant institutions of broader national life—Congress, the presidency, the Supreme Court, television news and newspapers, and big business—all saw sharp declines in high-trust responses (14% on average) and corresponding increases in low-trust responses (17% on average). Over half responded that they have little or no trust in Congress. Organized religion and banks also fared badly.

In short, the social fabric seems to have improved in home and neighbourhood, largely due to the modern policing and security apparatus, which leverages current capabilities for continuous electronic observation, as well as real-time tracking, parsing and synthesis of massive data. The broader institutions of representative government (including the Fourth Estate) and legitimacy, though, are a shambles.

The Cross

The subjective fragmentation of the modern world is old hat. The remarkable news is that the internet has also shattered the underlying unity of nature that had driven scientific progress since the apple dropped on Newton's noggin.

For an example of the old zeitgeist of seamless nature in juxtaposition to subjective fragmentation, consider the natural history museum as described by French anthropologist Philippe Descola (of whom much later) in *Beyond Nature and Culture*. The natural history museum, he remarks, consists of "huge ontological inventories arranged according to rules of systemic classification" decontextualized in their drawers, bins and so on, in such a way that the only relation that takes place is "one of general inclusion in the classificatory system." This is an arrangement true to the vision pioneered by Enlightenment classificatory geniuses such as Linnaeus, who concocted the system to begin with, and to doughty explorers who first plumbed the modern world, such as von Humboldt.

However, natural history museums also have ethnographical exhibits, presented in an utterly different way, as ambiguous places where classifications of all kinds—racial, linguistic, cultural, technological, geographical, and stylistic—overlap and intertwine and where culture and its products indicate their resistance to being set into an order dictated by the natural sciences.... Humans constitute a single species whose members are hardly distinguishable physically and are without question included in nature's great register, yet turn out to be differentiated in so many ways once one examines how they make use of the world and give it meaning. This singularity of theirs means that no relations are transferable; none provides a model that can be generalized to include both humans and nonhumans...

The problem with Descola's description is that you can almost smell dust and sense neglect, not just of the scores of specimen but the entire concept. Natural history museums have had to adapt in major, related ways to maintain a modicum of public relevance and the financial support that comes with it. They have focused on special exhibits for which the overriding objective and criterion is entertainment of children. And the collections have come out of their draws and bottles and into cyberspace. No one's first thought when wondering about, say, a tawny frogmouth or a Walckenaer's Studded Arkys is to go to a natural history museum to see it in its decontextualized classificatory order: you google it. And once you to, you are immediately treated to all kinds of detail and happenstance about the critter in question that anchor it within its general particularity, indeed within the particularity of the moment injected with your own subjectivities. Rather than capitulating to the spatial authority of the experts who laid out the museum, what goes in which box or glass in which drawer, cabinet, room, and wing, you can surf however you want, drilling down on whatever detail or association catches your eye, jumping back and forth between disparate species, or between the species and human affairs. These substitute realities reached their logical conclusion in the animation-heavy movie series *Night at the Museum*, in which various exhibits and objects at the New York Museum of Natural History and later the Smithsonian come alive in a jumbled way so that, for example, characters from a Western diorama help fight off dinosaurs. These magically reanimated characters then interact with the movie protagonists.

Linnaeus, were he alive, would be largely irrelevant today, despite the very long shadow he still casts over science. Biologists rarely focus on the big picture in a serious way. Consider the odyssey of one Brandon McDonald, a university biology professor, who set out to create a list of biology disciplines and sub-disciplines. It is 53 pages long and contains some 450 entries, starting with acarology, the study of mites, and ending with zootomy, specializing in the dissection and anatomy of animals. Professor McDonald developed his *Annotated List of Disciplines and Sub-Disciplines in the Biological Sciences* through diligent research on the internet and on-line literature databases, weeding down entries to ensure all were backed by either a learned society (e.g., Acarological Society of America), peer-reviewed journal, active research institute, conference, or university course. His effort was inspired by a student's question during the first lecture of an introductory biology course. In his initial response to the student the professor named some 20 major disciplines, and supposed the list would run to 100 or more. There was, however, apparently no such list available until he published his in 2008, despite the fact that introductory biology texts always start with a 'What is Biology?' chapter. Professor McDonald conceived of his list partly as a way to allay student anxiety about biology; it seems fair to surmise that he was not wholly successful in that regard. He concludes his presentation of the list by cautioning that "[t]he changing nature of science will demand continual vigilance of advancements and discoveries in the biological sciences as they relate to further diversifications of biological disciplines."

It is worth emphasizing that Professor McDonald exercised restraint and selectivity in his compilation. Diligent mapping of the email traffic between biologists in any particular sub-discipline would likely show it shattered into cliques and sub-groups. There are many more species of mites and ticks than acarologists to study them; around 48,000 species of mites alone have been described, with untold further species awaiting discovery. Each has its peculiar characteristics and habitat. Specialization within the field is the only viable way to fend off superficiality.

An editorial by Arturo Casadevall and Ferric Fang in the April 2014 edition of *Infection and Immunology* laments the 'microbiological archipelago':

> Microbiology is an unusual discipline in which scientists usually specialize by becoming experts on individual microbes. Many microbiologists begin and end their scientific lives working on the same organism and together with their colleagues form

intellectual islands that, when considered in aggregate, constitute a microbial archipelago. Hence, specialization in microbiology results in fields that are delineated by phylogenetic boundaries. Medical microbiology has spawned bacteriology, mycology, parasitology, and virology, and as each field advances, each, too, spawns subdisciplines that can become fields unto themselves. For example, virology has become subdivided into positive- and negative-strand viruses, HIV, and DNA viruses. Similarly, most experimental bacteriologists, mycologists, and parasitologists remain focused on single organisms, often for their entire careers. This translates into a preference for scientific meetings that focus on the organism of interest and has resulted in a proliferation of single-organism conferences that promote even more specialization as individuals embrace even narrower subthemes.

The metaphor of an archipelago is vivid, but does not quite do justice to the process. Microbiology is a fractal archipelago, islands within islands within islands, all the way down to individual organisms, with countless uninhabited micro-islands waiting to be discovered.

Enter celebrity microbiologist Dr J. Craig Venter, whose scientific expeditions aboard the yacht *Sorcerer II* evoked the travels of Banks and Darwin, albeit with a few differences. Venter's core project consisted of taking samples of the ocean water at more or less regular intervals, straining the microorganisms from the samples, and airlifting the culled and frozen residue to his Institute for Biological Energy Alternatives in Maryland. This is an effective means of biological discovery, with the pilot project netting at least 1,800 new species and over 1.2 million new genes, some 800 of which convert sunlight to energy. It is all about the genes. What the microorganisms are actually like in their physical bodies, actions, and habitats, is observationally irrelevant, except as inferred from the genetic material "in the form of software-generated hypotheses about mutational distances and their meaning," as Alain Pottage describes it in a 2006 article in *BioSocieties*.

The radical decontextualization of genes is not to create a virtual natural history museum. Instead, it allows the genetic material to be systematically tested in newly created, fit-for-purpose organisms. Raw genomes, Pottage notes, are processed—"extracted, fragmented, amplified and then recomposed into a set of plausible genomes"—and then spliced into other, easily cultured micro-organisms where the encoded proteins and enzymes can be expressed and studied. Such hybrid organisms are only created for genes of interest, such as photoreceptor genes, which may be useful in developing alternative energy sources, or ones that might be applied for carbon sequestration.

It is difficult to determine where the parallels to software (particularly open-source software) end and the overlaps begin in his endeavour. Genetic code resembles computer code, software modularization emulates the genetically engineered organism of convenience, and collaborative debugging recalls the systematic testing of hundreds or thousands of pre-screened genomes. 'Nature' becomes a means of testing whether applications 'run' from the standpoint of addressing the intended human needs and problems. The glue, to the extent that such glue exists, is the system, not external reality.

Don't Touch

Still not convinced of nature's fundamental fragmentation nowadays? Consider internet-era environmentalism.

It's hard to overstate how much environmentalism has changed since my youthful days, when the glistening image of earth from outer space was still fresh. Its meaning, even then, was as much about vulnerability as the technological achievements that yielded the photo, but the main source of that vulnerability was thermonuclear war with the USSR.

The Environmental Protection Agency, created in 1970, was new. Though the threats it faced soon receded from the tangible immediacy of the 1969 Cuyahoga River fire, they were still fairly specific and tractable. DDT in insecticides and mosquito repellent was linked to fragile eggshells and the survival of the Bald Eagle in particular. Aerosol sprays caused a hole in the ozone layer protecting earth from unabated sunshine. Love Canal showed how chemicals lurked beneath seemingly idyllic communities, Chernobyl and Three Mile Island the hazards of meltdown. Raw coal smoke from factories and power plants caused acid rain, killing fish and firs at formerly pristine ponds.

Conservationism, the idea of preserving natural resources for the long-term benefit of man, by and large still guided the relations of people with natural places. Wilderness experiences were an unmediated encounter with the wholeness of nature, as an antidote to the subjective fragmentation of civilization.

Nowadays everything is threatened. The threats are to be met through determined balkanization of the natural world, quarantining the various bits from humankind. A few anecdotes illustrate the point. Not so long ago my wife and I visited Birdland, a vast avian zoo in Singapore. It holds a pod of penguins in artificial deep freeze, but mostly has tropical birds from around the world in open-air cages and apiaries. Each fowl has its information plaque, and the route around the park is seeded with didactic material, but we came away with little understanding of the birds themselves. The plaques followed but a general pattern, offering a map of the region where that type of bird is found (in thick red outline) and a colour gauge registering the threat it faced, from green for no threat (included on the gauge for theoretical completeness) to red (highly endangered). The didactic material focused on human menace to birds in their habitat, from illegal pet trade to lumbering and agriculture. My wife and I initially found this irritating –

we really did want to know something about the birds themselves – but then realized that the overriding message and meaning of Birdland *was* the patchwork matrix of territory and vulnerability. That was what nature had become, essentially.

Not long after we visited Cradle Mountain National Park in the highlands of Tasmania. We found mile after mile of boardwalks stretching across the red heathlands and boggy alpine meadows, designed to prevent any direct contact between visitors and nature. In more remote areas the construction of the boardwalks had required helicopter logistics. It was impressive and beautiful in a way, the weathered, grey-white planks snaking across the land like one of Cristo's artworks. One boardwalk reached nearly to the steep tumbles of gigantic boulders below the dolomite summit of Cradle Mountain itself. It ended at a building with toilets. The signage inside informed that the helicopter also did honey-wagon duty, and instructed us as to just what we were allowed to throw in and what to carry out. At the Visitors' Center (which we quirkily visited just before leaving) a film loop intoned that a clump of moss could take 30 years to recover from a single footprint. The old Woodsman's Ethic—'Take Only a Photo, Leave Only a Footprint'—

effectively had been replaced with 'Stay on Boardwalk, Take Selfies.'

From Cradle Mountain we headed south to Lake St. Clair National Park, stopping by the Ranger's Station in preparation to climb Mt. Rufus. Outside the doorway was a bulletin board with mugshots of wildflowers. A ranger came out with more pictures to tack up. We asked him where to go to see the Small Bird Orchid. "I wouldn't have any idea," he said, "but there's a Facebook page called Tasmanian Orchids you can check out. You can see it there." We were, in fact, already looking at a picture of it. We asked him if the webpage gave GPS coordinates for the flowers, and he looked at us like we were crazy. "No, they just tell the park where people were when they saw it."

Fragmented though nature is, the bits are held in place by overarching menace. That menace, though, cannot be apprehended directly by humans, but only through computer models that run into the double-dilemma of imprecision and speculation. Earth science in recent decades has been pushed out of its historical mission of interpreting overdetermined, site-specific phenomenon across the geological eons. It has been forced into the uncomfortable role of predicting disasters emerging from complex systems, where by and large the interests of policy makers lie, with public funds following. While the ultimate goal is to make disasters behave like computer applications, this coincidence is, for the foreseeable future, elusive in terms of the actual timing and severity of events. The applications instead marry emulation of past natural behaviour with simulations of the future, making qualitative or statistical generalizations across simulations while staying vague about timing and place. The unpredictability of events is what makes the earth history so interesting, but the lack of precision is problematic from the public and policy-maker viewpoint. Big science is thus throwing ever-larger amounts of computer power into the quest for greater granularity.

The expanding scientific industry of modelling climate and weather epitomizes the dilemma, having led, in recent decades, to three largely incompatible, yet pervasive, paradigms of modern thought. The apocryphal butterfly effect expresses incommensurateness and the irrelevance of proximity in cause and effect. Daisy World poses the earth as a self-regulating system, whereby ostensibly minute adaptive changes (small shifts in the odds that a flower will be white or black) counteract disturbances to the system. Global climate change blankets a host of evils ranging from slowly rising sea levels and droughts to storms and landslides, all linked to concentrating CO_2 in the atmosphere. Given this wealth of options, the hermeneutics of future interpretation are informed by social values, making it susceptible to herd mentality and considerations of prestige and finance.

Massive resources for ever-more complex data gathering and computing efforts have, so far, not yielded much improvement in predictive accuracy. The effort clearly still has a ways to run, and indeed might be extended indefinitely. Professor Tim Palmer, who specializes in modelling and predicting climate at Oxford, opines in a November 2014 article in *Nature* that the problem with current models is that they use a cell resolution of 100 kilometres, too large to capture small-scale processes such as local cloud systems, which must be 'parameterized'. These fudge factors are the main source of the stubborn systemic errors and inaccuracy in the climate models. The solution is to build a simulator with one-kilometre resolution, extrapolating the earth's weather down to the individual cloud. A one-century simulation at such granularity would only need a budget of a few hundred million euros a years, exascale computers, and hardware capable of allowing computers to share and archive the millions of variables and data. Even that model, though, would require parameterization of cloud processes such as turbulence, droplets and ice crystals. Exascale computers, which do not exist, would be 50 times faster than current supercomputers. The current target is to have them online by 2023.

Assuming away the difficulties of creating Professor Palmer's dream and the sub-cloud inaccuracy that would persist, such simulations would still require assumptions as to the future course of human activity and technology. These are inherently unknowable, and create the entanglement of including Professor Palmer and his colleagues (along with the rest of us and a few future unborn generations) within the system he purports to design and control. Indeed, the primary purpose of building such a model would not be to produce accurate climate forecasts but rather inaccurate ones, galvanizing and equipping humankind with the means to avoid the planetary plague of disasters. Ultimately, that is, such models are not about studying the natural environment at all, but rather a cybernetic means to steer a real world in which the distinction between nature and culture has lost relevance. Science thus not only survives the demise of its foundational assumption; it thrives in its absence. The horizon of his efforts is not the model, nor the climate, but society itself, scripted through the development and application of the model, the social meaning of its simulations, and the claims of legitimacy it confers.

The Boxer

Specific applications of computer and communications technology for policing, gene prospecting, climatological prediction, and so on have been a factor in either curbing social entropy or fragmenting physical reality. The role of internet-era technology, though, is deeper and more general that these examples suggest. It is the boxer himself, delivering the cross and jab.

Its pugilist role owes to its abiding qualities as medium and message. Internet communication commingles individual subjectivity with external code, a special ambiguity in which the interior fragmentation of humans is simultaneously enabled, extended and controlled through linkages. Fragmented thinking is accommodated and encouraged but curbed at the extremes, allowing users to graduate interaction with others while outsourcing integration and direction. It continually poses a dilemma of split physical reality, compelling navigation between external realms. This characteristic reaches its purest expression in the cutting-edge technology of virtual reality.

No One Knows

Internet-era communication is ambiguous, meaning it is de-contextualized from the physical circumstances of sender and receiver. A *New Yorker* cartoon several years ago (still available online at the Condé Nast Collection) featured a dog seated at a computer, with the caption, "On the Internet, no one knows you are a dog." People apply this insight by using smartphones in incongruous situations: over half of Americans while driving, a third at a movie theatre, on a dinner date or at a child's school function, and around 10% in the shower or during sex, according to a June 2013 poll by Harris Interactive.

My wife recently got a computer and had some problems configuring the software, so we ended up chatting online with a technician. The communication was so scripted and stilted, the bonhomie so obviously faked, the end of the session so weirdly disjointed, and the lack of any real information about the counterpart so evident that I initially thought it might be a chatbot, just a computer program designed to emulate a person. But Microsoft was still using real people. The experience inevitably brought to mind the Turing test, Alan Turing's famous argument that if people can't tell if they are talking to a person or a machine, then machines can think. The Turing Test has motivated development of Artificial

Intelligence ever since he posed it in 1950. Turing may not have contemplated that the computers might pass the test not because they start acting like people, but rather because people start acting like computers.

A simple model of communication is: sender → message → receiver. Ambiguity gives the message autonomy from context or intention. This does not mean that messages fly about randomly. Rather, they are classified and categorized, through a mix of intention and happenstance, by the affinities and links that constitute an online network. That network of accumulating content, addresses and permissions is subject to further organization, partly ad hoc and partly automatic, through searching. The related content, targeted advertising, automated responses and profiling that ensue from searching extend and alter the network and the meaning of the messages.

The autonomy of the message, though, does not mean that two ends of the communication, sender and receiver, fade away like the Cheshire Cat. They instead both begin to acquire the characteristics, transient and permanent, of content and linkages that have moved partially beyond either one's control. This process is shown in the following diagram, which follow the simple one but shows what it has become:

Meatspace   Cyberspace   Meatspace

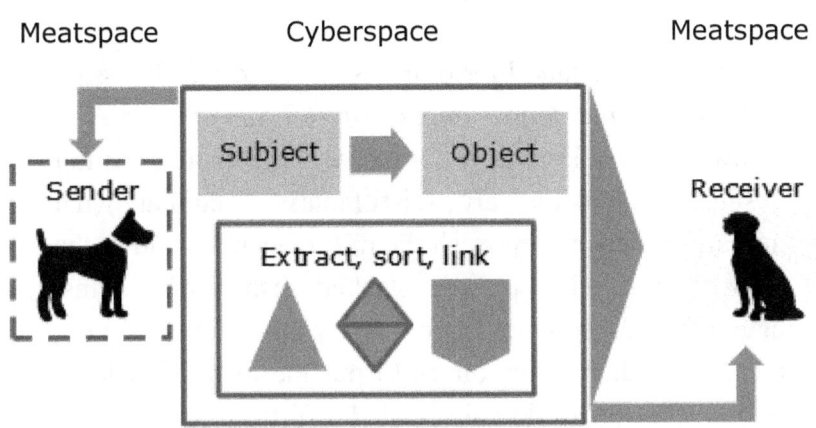

There are two main categories of linkages in this diagram. The first is within cyberspace, where the extracting, sorting, and joining of content associates and extends the meaning of even the most banal communication. The message is part of a thread; it is stored, and becomes susceptible to forwarding, searching, and retrieving; it contains links to webpages and blogs. It may be generated autonomously in response to actions that were ostensibly self-contained. Its contents are perused by bots who then communicate back as though they were people.

But activity in cyberspace is also linked to the identity of those who corporeally remain in what, for want of a better antonym, I will accede to calling meatspace. Perhaps the best way to grasp this is by building on a dishwasher analogy, proposed by the philosopher of information Luciano Floridi in his September 2006 essay, *A look into the future impact of ICT on our lives*. A dishwasher is a kind of robot for washing dishes, but not designed, as in some naïve sci-fi fantasy, to emulate what humans do when they wash them. It does not stand at the kitchen sink, pick up the stacked dishes with arms, manipulate them under the hot water and onto the drying rack. Instead, it relies on us to put the dishes inside it, into a controlled domain sealed off from the outside world, where it can do the work of washing efficiently.

One could imagine a dishwasher designed to make inferences about the people outside its box based on the number and variety of dishes, food residue and frequency, timing and so on. With further imagination, dishwashers could be linked and share data, so that the inferences made are based not just on information available to an individual dishwasher, but on that of the whole network. Finally, one can imagine inferences by the robot collective within its hermetic domain about its owners impacting how the latter live their lives on the outside: what food they buy, medical attention and insurance, whom they socialize with and how; and in turn the people on the outside making inferences about in-washer activity, and engaging in more complex relationships with their machine and through it with others.

This final state of affairs, the full realization of the vision and potential of robots that wash dishes, captures the second level of linkages, pairing entities that are fundamentally unlike because they pertain to separate and different domains, changing the meaning of both.

The fact that people have no issues communicating via smartphones while engaged in sex or showering can be taken as evidence that the inference of the characteristics of sender and receiver based on the message is, in principle, pretty wildly inaccurate. It could also be argued that the characterizations are accurate, but only within the virtual domain in which they occur. But it could just as well be argued that the character of sex, showers and messages are all being fundamentally altered, though not in ways that can readily be shared.

Anonymous, the largely spontaneous hacker-activist group that contributed to the downfall of the Ben Ali regime in Tunisia, has a tight, globalized on-line counter-culture, centring (as Gabriella Coleman advises in *Hacker, Hoaxer, Whistleblower, Spy*) on 'lulz,' or doing things for the hell of it, avoidance of 'faggotry' or self-aggrandisement, and a half-facetious braggadocio that readily turns into cyber-attacks. Offline its members have included inter alia a sixteen-year-old middle-class Londoner of Iraqi origin, a Puerto Rican living in a high-rise public housing project in New York, an Irish chemistry student whose father had been jailed for involvement in the IRA, a Scotsman from the Isle of Yell, and a British war vet who posed as a female online. Which ones are real? To what degree are they separate or conjoined? Does the internet make them more or less fragmented? Is the fragmentation subjective, physical, or both?

Following on *The New Yorker*, I meant the use of dogs at either end of the diagram to be funny, because of the incongruity between the mental world of dogs and the operations of cyberspace. Replacing dogs with humans blurs the lines between cyberspace and the minds of sender and receiver. The two have converged in the infinite yet organized cacophony of engineered linkages.

Rise of the fragmented

The ambiguity and linkages that characterize internet communications and alter individual subjectivity should be viewed in the context of the affinity of computers for people with autism spectrum disorder.

ASD, which includes both autism and Asperger's, is a creature of the computer age. Autism didn't make it into the American Psychiatric Association's *Diagnostic and Statistical Manual of Mental Disorders*, the canonical reference guide for mental ailments, until 1980. Asperger's syndrome was included in 1994. Accordingly to the Centers for Disease Control and Prevention, a US public health institute, in the 1980s about one in 2000 (0.05% of the population) was diagnosed with autism; now one in 68 (1.4%) has ASD. The rates of diagnosis vary widely, up to a South Korean study that found one in 38 (or 2.6% of the population) with the condition.

Computers are used widely to treat ASD people. There is something about the nature of the interface and interaction that can engage them, breaking the shell of isolation or taming inner demons. The initial attraction may be visual integration, with the small, tight microcosm of the computer interface at least partially mitigating the tendency of ASD people to see the world in disjointed fragments. This helps them to concentrate, upon which they discover the computer's ability to serve as a controlled and safe means of graduated communication. They then experience the computer as a medium in which they can find success, however limited at first, with the corresponding boost to self-respect. As described in a fact sheet by autismhelp.org, a virtuous cycle of learning ensues, improving visual tracking, spatial analysis and synthesis, memory, planning and organization, hand-eye coordination, and problem solving.

Many people with ASD work in IT, with German software giant SAP AG going so far, as a March 27, 2014 article in *The Wall Street Journal* notes, as to actively recruit people with autism to debug software. The overlap between geekdom and ASD has bred suggestions that everyone from Bill Gates, Steve Jobs and Mark Zuckerberg down is somewhere on the spectrum. Temple Grandin, a remarkable autistic scientist, is quoted in a May 2014 article in *FT Wealth* claiming that Silicon Valley is chock full of 'happy Aspies'. These titbits, though, are not discernibly reflected in official diagnostic statistics. California does not have a particularly high incidence of ASD diagnosis. The areas where the IT industry is concentrated do have much higher rates of diagnosis than the rest of the state, but this correlates to parents' education and not profession. When they intermarry, California geeks are not especially likely to have children who are diagnosed with ASD. This is partly because diagnostic standards are more rigorous in California than some other parts of the US. More rigorous states like California could be missing a lot of borderline cases, or less rigorous states could be making a lot of false diagnoses.

But the fuzzy data point also to the mercurial nature of the malady. There are dramatic differences in behaviour and ability across the spectrum, notably in IQ. No single behaviour establishes the condition. It is instead a matter of judging how well individuals fit a general pattern. More broadly, it is also a matter of determining whether the general pattern constitutes an illness, inasmuch as the character of ailments in general, and those that have to do with the mind in particular, are strongly determined by the society in which they are experienced. Society constitutes mental conditions as illnesses mostly because a set of behaviours is seen as directly or indirectly contagious, a moral or physical menace, and/or a condition treatable by procedures as well as resources. Autism and Asperger's were created as much as 'discovered' when they were included in the *Diagnostic and Statistical Manual of Mental Disorders*.

Why has ASD incidence exploded? A lot of explanatory effort has aimed at a comforting counterfactual, that if we had been as enlightened back then as we are now, we would have detected similar levels of ASD, so today's supposed higher incidence is just a measurement problem. But the counterfactual of retrospective ASD diagnosis studies is not, as such efforts suggest, a question of mentally transporting current diagnostic capability back in time. It is transporting our current society back in time.

A lot of "normal" people probably also fit on the spectrum; it's just that they inhabit the infrared part. The stereotypical geek with an uncanny grasp of code and systems and limited social skills in the flesh may haunt the border regions, issues fading in and out of sight, a fully functioning – indeed thriving – member of our strange new world.

And just as the full spectral range exceeds the subset diagnosed with ASD, so the affinities between the condition and computers extend beyond their overtly therapeutic application. It would be misleading to present computers merely as a kind of doorway or window through which ASD people can enter or regard the world at large. Rather, the structure and exercise of communications technology resembles ASD, leaving plenty of flexibility and incentive for non-ASD people edge toward the ASD patterns of cognition. This is perhaps easiest to understand with the overtly social aspects of the technology, serving to connect two people physically located in meatspace. The capacity to regulate the degree and intensity of interaction, with the progressive tendency toward higher levels of engagement and contact, brings to mind the 'squeeze machine' that the young Temple Grandin invented first to substitute for, and then to assimilate, human contact. As she describes in "My Experiences with Visual Thinking Sensory Problems and Communication Difficulties"

> I craved deep pressure stimulation, but I pulled away and stiffened when my overweight aunt hugged me. In my two books, I describe a squeeze machine I constructed to satisfy my craving for the feeling of being held. The machine was designed so that I could control the amount and duration of the pressure. It was lined with foam rubber and applied pressure over a large area of my body. Gradually I was able to tolerate the machine holding me. The over sensitivity of my nervous system was slowly reduced. A stimulus that was once overwhelming and aversive had now become pleasurable. Using the machine enabled me to tolerate another person touching me.

A particularly acute example of the electronic equivalent of the squeeze machine is internet dating and matchmaking sites, which are a boon to those who feel socially vulnerable, or confused by the ins and outs of feminism, coquetry, harassment and rejection, or yearn romantically for a kindred soul or object of fantasy unavailable in their current meatspace. Breaking up, the old song says, is hard to do, but easier and less damaging by internet. Often, of course, the initial virtual relationship is rapidly redomained, at least partially, into meatspace. In other cases, the virtual relationship is all there is for months and months as the counterparts gain confidence in themselves and each other.

A second major convergence is integration of cognitive fragments into coherence. In the diagram of communications I highlighted both autonomous linkages, within the message, and those of identity between it and the sender and receiver in meatspace. The slap-dash piling of linkages and non-linear and emergent process of ordering also parallel the autistic way of thinking. In her personal account of "How does visual thinking work in the mind of a person with autism?" for the *Philosophical Transactions of the Royal Society*, Grandin uses the jigsaw puzzle analogy that is emblematic for autistics, but it is a puzzle assembled by examining individual pieces, with no guiding senses of the overall image that will emerge, until the project is well advanced. She invokes explicitly cybernetic comparisons. Her mind is like a search engine for images, her imagination a virtual reality program, her mind's eye a computer monitor. All the linkages and categories emerge gradually, non-sequentially, from the ground up. She brings us back to the unexpected resolution of Alan Turing's test for

Artificial Intelligence, with the confusion of humans and computers occurring when the former come to resemble the latter. The interchangeability offers a cognitive variation on the squeeze machine, with the same dynamic of control, limitation and progressive mastery. Users, ASD or not, can choose to be anywhere on a spectrum that ranges from outsourcing the brain's work of linkage and association to providing a domain for the realization of its full internal capacity.

Most online learning, which is to say, a large amount of all learning nowadays, particularly for adults, occurs through cooperative effort between minds and technology. People often begin with only a vague idea of what they want to know, make an initial assay, peruse the results and refine the search. The search engine learns with them, providing better and more focused searches and suggestions in response to the user's own responses, even as the user gains mastery and uses his own memory and experience, aided by stored 'favourites,' downloaded documents, and the processing of information received into other products. Even the free version of the photo app Flickr has a 'friendly robot' that performs reconnaissance on the user's images to propose an emergent tag-word structure.

The final area of ASD-computer convergence is in execution and control. The same range of user responses, from outsourcing to empowerment, characterizes both the challenges and condition of ASD people and the basic dilemma and privilege faced by all users. Grandin visualizes her brain as a corporate office building where the telephone and computer connections from the president (frontal cortex) to the departments are poor, but the 'technical nerd departments' are exceptionally powerful, and better at processing detailed information. Her analogy may already be slightly dated. Online nowadays, the frontal cortex has begun to outsource executive functions to the other side of the digital interface. The office at the top of the building may not just have computer connections; it might be the computer.

An ostensibly trivial example comes from healthcare. A colleague of mine wears a wristband that monitors his movement and heartrate during the day, and transmits the data into the web, where it is monitored by his insurance company. If he meets mandated objectives for daily walking, he gets a break on his insurance premium. He generally meets his objectives, because he is walking for the band and the vast, intangible world behind it.

One of the great things about internet-era technology is that it has empowered a section of society that might otherwise have been marginalized. But it has also marginalized a very broad swathe of society, like a fish out of water, in non-internet society. When the system goes down, or our assigned hardware malfunctions, for example, our immediate inclination, with listlessness or frustration, is to stop work. This is not merely because we are denied the tools for work, but because our capacity for self-direction is compromised, in an interesting way that raises the question of what that 'self' really is. Parents wrestling with the unruly emergence of adolescent identity have a boon: confiscating their offspring's interfaces is as effective as grounding ever was.

Virtual Reality

Mostly we get by with a surprisingly narrow connection to cyberspace: somewhere between the few square inches our smart phones display and the flat-screen monitors on our desks. A vanguard area of technology attacks this weakness, developing interfaces that effectively gobble up the physical body in what is known as virtual reality. This is wondrous, but has a dystopic downside that was captured in a 1999 sci-fi movie, *The Matrix*, which in turn restated the old philosophical dilemma of the brain in a vat. If utterly immersive and convincing realities can be manufactured, quite independently of what is 'really' there, how will we know? How would we be sure that what we take for reality is not actually the (malign) manipulation of who/whatever creates and subjects us to the simulated environment?

But of course we do keep track of what's going on. Even within the totalizing apparatus, experiencing virtual reality, adults remain aware that another reality is also there, ostensibly less real, but also in a way more real, and occupying more or less the same time and space. Orientation within the technological virtuosity of virtual reality thus means buying into a notion of fragmented physical reality, two dissimilar ones present at once, one of which we assign a set of ontological traits under the rubric of virtuality, the other those of 'real' reality.

The Virtual Human Interaction Lab, under the auspices of the Department of Communication at Stanford University, takes as its mission to understand what happens to people, individually and particularly as they interact with others, in virtual reality. In pursuit of that mission it develops its own virtual-reality technologies, including gesture tracking, three-dimensional modelling, and agent-behaviour algorithms.

The Lab, however, cannot resist the temptation to move beyond behavioural study to applications of virtual reality that are intended to curb the threats of fragmentation. These include having participants "viscerally embody an avatar who encounters various forms of racism" and other initiatives to promote empathy with the disadvantaged and different, as well as virtual experiences to induce environmentally friendly behaviours such as such as using less paper and hot water. "Gas-guzzling" cars and energy inefficient homes are on the agenda. Extending the empathy theme across the species barrier, one can inhabit a fish avatar, and thus be guided to heighted awareness of and concern for acidifying oceans.

The flip side of the coin of physical fragmentation, in other words, is an aggressive program to contain subjective fragmentation. The doubly fragmented world of virtual reality jointly gropes toward wholeness and continuity, which becomes yet a third type of half-illusion.

II. INTERNET SOCIETY SANS INTERNET

The train of thought I have just laid out, in strict chronological truth, has the cart before the horse. It began while reading *Beyond Nature and Culture*, the aforementioned tome by anthropologist Philippe Descola. All this business so far about the fragmented subjectivity of society, fragmented nature, and the persistent nudging of internet-era technology, is largely his fault.

I make this confession not just to shift the blame, but also to share some of the shock with which I realized that it is possible to have an internet society without the internet. The ontological pickle we inhabit, subjectively *and* physically fragmented but not falling apart, is not unique to our civilization. Other societies were, in their own ways, no less information-rich, and had similar baggage. It's as if we were adopted as babies and then as adults met our biological siblings for the first time. Cool, but weird.

In *Beyond Nature and Culture*, Professor Descola developed a scheme for sorting the world's societies, which he boils down to a two-by-two matrix. The axes of his matrix reflect what, he argues, is a basic human duality between body and self: the sense that there is a unified something, associated with and carried within us, but different from and in some way separable from the outer physical form and its perceivable activities. In western cultures we think of body and soul, or body and mind. These dualities have often been criticized as ethnocentric, and of course in a way they are. But they should be thought of as specific renderings of a distinction that all human societies make in one way or another between physical and interior.

He argues that experienced relations depend on the a priori ontological statuses we assign. We classify things within a broader category based on some common characteristics, so that, for example, an igloo, a bungalow, a mansion and even a cave may be given an ontological category of *house*. This categorization is so basic and automatic that it is difficult to accommodate perception and language without it. We are also going to assign that category a basic status of likeness or apartness, similarity or dissimilarity. Continuing with the example, we might see the house as containing a spirit (a haunted house, or local god or ancestors in various cultures), being physically linked to its inhabitants (a physical extension of their selves, at the extreme as rendered in Poe's short story *The Fall of the House of Usher*), or having a special character of belongingness, as a home. Or we might see it as just some materials fashioned in a particular way.

The basis for similarity or dissimilarity can be based on either physical or interior qualities, or both. Whether the linkages exist and what they consist of are not innate to the things themselves. They instead are mostly projected upon them. And of course, what we project in turn depends critically on the norms, institutions and so on that have socialized us and continue to reinforce and allow us to function within our society. There must be common patterns within a society for fundamental ontological categories, distinctions and assignments.

The critical step in Descola's argument is to assert that the ontological assignments of similarity and dissimilarity to the internal and physical aspects of the things to which humans relate are not case by case or even across the world's societies. Rather, societies show systematic tendencies toward a specific type of ontological identification.

His matrix lays out the options for overarching modes of ontological identification. It juxtaposes interior similarity and dissimilarity (the vertical axis) against physical similarity and dissimilarity (the horizontal axis). There are four resulting combinations, consequently four modes, and four basic types of society. Animist societies see physical dissimilarity but internal similarity; Totemic societies both physical and internal similarity; Naturalist societies physical similarity but internal dissimilarity;

and Analogist societies both physical and internal dissimilarity.

The first two types of society in Descola's classification have familiar labels and are far from the Western mainstream, so I can dispatch with them in fairly short order. The basic idea of animism, that things have an underlying commonality of spirit despite ostensive differences, entails a projection of culture onto the natural world, so that animals and plants have their own esoteric societies not unlike ours, and relations between them must be handled in ways not dissimilar to those between human communities. Mythology revolves around making the esoteric commonality explicit, and is full of interspecies relations conducted in very human terms, including marriages and ambiguous mixed-species hybrids at home in both societies. Magic and religion often involve one's spirit taking a totally different form, and hunting is seen as a complex matter, akin to seduction at the level of prey and involving protracted, reciprocal negotiations at the level of the respective communities.

Totemic societies discern underlying commonality at physical and interior levels between the people and the totem, and the segmentation cuts across nature and culture with no particular distinction between them. The main examples of totemic societies are among aboriginal

Australians. Aboriginal societies revolve around Dreamtime, which has characteristics of both a primordial and paradigmatic time of creation as well as an alternative plane available here and now. The distinguishing characteristic of Dreamtime is the complete obviousness of the pervasive commonality of totemic object and the people of the totem, and by orienting everything to Dreamtime the physical differences Westerners observe between, say, kangaroos and people can be reduced to mere superficialities, while rules for interaction apply indiscriminately to both. Aboriginal societies do make major distinctions, but these concern the relations between the various human-totem fusions.

The modern West, in Descola's view, is a third type of society—naturalist—deriving its character from a hard distinction between nature and culture. The world of nature, including human beings to the extent that humans are merely natural creatures, is essentially continuous, composed of the same matter, subject to the same controlling laws of science and differing only by degrees of complexity and particular niches occupied. Culture pertains explicitly to human society, and is a source of absolute differentiation between the human and non-human worlds, as well as irreducible heterogeneity between the different human groups themselves. In biblical terms, only humans have souls and God gave us dominion over the things of the world, but the curse of Babel is upon us.

Analogist societies, the final option, see commonality at neither a physical nor an interior level. This sounds intolerable, so Descola hastens to clarify that the gaps and distances in such societies are small. That is to say, there is almost physical commonality, but not quite, and almost interior commonality, but always room to doubt. These societies thus orient themselves by means of analogy—analogy being a lower standard of certainty than proof—and engage in a great deal of hermeneutic disputation within a cosmology that forcibly relates everyday existence to an overarching framework. Such societies can be quite complex. His major examples include traditional Hindu and Chinese society, as well as the pre-modern West in the period ending roughly in the Newtonian revolution at the end of the seventeen century.

His definition of analogism is

> a mode of identification that divides up the whole collection of existing beings into a multiplicity of essences, forms, and substances separated by small distinctions and sometimes arranged on a graduated scale

so that it becomes possible to recompose the system of initial contrasts into a dense network of analogies that link together the intrinsic properties of the entities that are distinguished in it.... In short, analogy is a hermeneutic dream of plenitude that arises out of a sense of dissatisfaction. Noting that the general segmentation of the world's components is based on a scale of small differences, it nurtures the hope of weaving these slightly heterogeneous elements into a web of meaningful affinities and attractions that gives the appearance of constituting a continuity. All the same, the ordinary state of the world is one of differences infinitely multiplied, while resemblance is the hoped-for means of making that world intelligible and bearable.

His words are, inadvertently, a fair summary of life lived on and through the internet.

Professor Descola details the characteristics of analogism, referring to other societies that ostensibly are culturally distant, and certainly are less technologically accomplished, than ours, particularly focusing on the example of the Nahua (Aztecs) of Mesoamerica. Some of the characteristics amount to a psychology of disintegration, compensatory mechanisms partly offsetting the disorientation of fragmented reality. Others constitute a practical cybernetics, how things get done amidst the bits and pieces. I find them all in contemporary society, and not limited, as Descola suggests, to horoscope watchers and New Age sects. They are mainstream. Internet-era technology is involved throughout. Some characteristics are merely computer-enabled, others of the essence of the technology, almost imposed by it.

Analogy sums up these characteristics, but with an adjustment in emphasis from normal usage. Analogy normally consists of relating ostensibly different things to each other, so that the one that is better understood explains the other. The purpose is to improve understanding, and after that occurs, the link can be discarded. But it can also be an understanding of ostensibly different things with the overriding purpose of sustaining the linkage, so that the estrangement is attenuated, avoiding the risk of disorientation and corresponding impossibility of purposeful action. The analogies of analogical societies are of this second kind.

Descola's classification of modern society as naturalist is dated. In the new millennium it has shifted back to analogism.

Psychology of Disintegration

The psychology of disintegration features beings that guide fortune and destiny, constructs to coordinate individual plurality, poles of hot and cold, macrocosmic correspondences, preoccupation with genealogy and sacrifice.

Influential beings

Descola notes that in analogical societies

> the quest for well-being or for the causes of misfortune is based on the hypothesis that the qualities, movements, and structural modifications of certain existing beings exert an influence on the destiny of humans or are themselves influenced by the behaviour of those humans. This obsession... is affirmed with a vigour that becomes increasingly manic the more its effects are reputed to be crucial.

His description, of course, matches God, who despite the intervening distances and differences bears more than a little resemblance to us and hears and responds to our prayers, at minimum dropping us clues as to what we should do. That God has made quite a comeback in recent decades, confounding predictions in the 1980s that the trend toward secularism was irreversible.

But it also sounds like national governments, to whom we vote rather than pray. These have distanced themselves while increasing their control. The distancing is evident in the demographics of representation. In the US, for example, the size of the House of Representatives was capped at 435 in 1929 under the Permanent Apportionment Act. At the time each representative stood for 164,000 potential voters, a number that had just doubled with the addition of women to the electorate. Now each represents 545,000. The dilution is far greater for senators, who were fixed at two per state from the start. In 1790, when the ink on the Constitution was still drying, each senator on average represented about 38,000 citizens. The current average is 2,352,000, and in more populous states (e.g., California, population 38.8 million) the number is much higher. In parallel, federalism has become hollow. Federal grants to state and local governments grew from essentially nothing in 1960 to $628 billion in 2015, marking the steady extension of the central government's grasp. The extension of central government control is often asserted under its constitutional right to regulate interstate commerce. Almost anything, it turns out, may have some implication for interstate commerce, if you think about it hard enough.

Descola's description matches our markets too, which we (in Marx's primitivist turn of phrase) fetishize as a matter of course, converting a loosely defined domain of human institutions and endeavours into a semi-autonomous being that influences and controls us, yet remains at least partly susceptible to us. Anybody who deals with traders or follows business press should be familiar with the phenomenon: it is difficult to imagine the daily functioning of the economy without it. Friedrich Hayek makes it a cornerstone of his defence of markets, as against his bugaboo central planning, notably in his 1945 classic article *The Use of Knowledge in Society*. Before him of course, was Adam Smith's celebrated "invisible hand", although in Smith's case, writing circa 1776, it was just a figure of speech.

Such markets are often half-mirages, of fairly recent appearance. Take for example, oil, the king of commodities, where there was nothing approaching a world market until about 1988. Such a market now exists, but its actual workings illustrate how far from the mark a fetishized rendering can be. The main worldwide benchmark for oil is Brent, which ostensibly refers to oil produced from the Brent field in the North Sea. Brent is actually an index of crudes in which the original Brent field itself long ago ceased to be an important component. Shell is now decommissioning the Brent field; when it finishes Brent will have no Brent. The components of the Brent index are regularly adjusted to take into account changes in the production of fields. Prices are created and divulged on an ongoing basis by the employees of price reporting agencies, Platts and Argus, as a business.

The market for Brent is almost entirely paper and derivatives, in which hedgers, traders and speculators are key participants. Crudes making up the overwhelming majority of the world's oil supply, such as those from the Middle East, are priced on an explicit differential (i.e., upward or downward adjustment in dollars per barrel) to the Brent benchmark. They have no liquid market of their own. Platts and Argus employees continually tweak the reported price of Brent based on their assessment of movements in the traded Brent market index itself and the differentials that mark physical crude transactions.

Coordination of plurality

Descola observes:

> The dominant feature... of any analogical
> system, is the grouping within every existing
> entity of a plurality of aspects the right

> coordination of which is believed to be
> necessary for the stabilization of that entity's
> individual identity, for the exercise of its
> facilities and dispositions, and for the
> development of a mode of being in
> accordance with its 'nature'.... Every
> existing being is different from every other
> on account of the plurality of its components
> and the diverse modes of their combination.

Though Descola had in mind the complex theory of humans held by the Nahuas, he also poses the problem of modern identity. The need to find one's "right" identity, in accordance with one's unique nature, is part of becoming an adult in our society, and has been at least since. Erikson's identity psychology and Maslow's hierarchy of needs found fertile ground in US campuses during the 1970s and 1980s. My undergraduate years in the '80s were largely an effort to discover what I wanted to do, with the general goal of self-actualization. The presumption was that a job would follow. Subsequent generations, relentlessly assured of their personal uniqueness since before conscious memories begin, have seen the importance of identity only grow.

The search for individual identity meshes with the diversification of labour. Work in our thoroughly organic society means developing certain faculties applied within a specific domain, with practical procedures, techniques, tools and machines adapted for that particular purpose. Specialization in turn creates minor chasms between those practicing other occupations. In *The Gifts of Athena* (2002), the economic historian Joel Mokyr points out that practical knowledge is largely background skills and understanding, with explicit instructions or recipes containing only a fraction of information needed for the task at hand. Explicit knowledge may even be superfluous. A colleague of mine recalls the shock he felt as a young civil engineer when workers ignored the blueprints when laying rebar for a bridge; they just got on with the task at hand. He soon discovered that they did not know how to read blueprints. Conversely, reading blueprints does not mean you can lay rebar.

Hot and cold

Descola continues:

> Another way of imparting order and meaning to a world full of singularities is to distribute these into great inclusive structures that stretch between two poles. In this way, the teeming mass of attributes can be contained by an operation of classification into a simplified nomenclature of perceptible qualities. Two such nomenclatures are very

common: that which opposes the hot and the cold and, sometimes combined with these, that which opposes the dry and the wet. In fact, these perhaps constitute the most obvious indications of an analogical ontology.

He particularly has in mind Nahua dualism. But our society also moves within a polarity of hot and cold, with hot denoting sexual attractiveness and cold asexuality. People warm up when they are sexually aroused, of course, but our hot/cold distinction is only weakly based on the observed surface temperatures of passion and disinterest. Rather, it is derived from the intermittent sexuality of other animals. With apologies for bluntness, when we say a girl is "hot" we analogize between her and a bitch in heat. It is interesting and paradoxical, given our simultaneous emphasis on gender equality, that this is a high complement. It no longer applies just to women. Guys can be hot, and this is also a complement to them.

Year-around sexuality and the unobviousness of times when women are fertile rank just below language, upright posture and opposable thumbs as distinctive traits of Homo sapiens. There is thus a sense in which the analogical adoption of obvious and intermittent sexuality is a denial of our humanness. Particularly since the advent of the Pill people in general, and women in particular, have gained control over their sexuality, at least insofar as its reproductive consequences. Being by nature able to reproduce at any time of the year, women now by and large choose when they are fertile, using our technological prowess to become more dog-like.

Sexual liberation, combined with the impersonality of modern society and the movement of women into non-traditional roles, have created a parallel need for sexual attraction to be regulated. There are times when a woman wants to be sexually attractive and times when she does not and times when a man can behave sexually towards her and times when he can't, and vice versa. Confusing the times invites a sharp rebuff or charges of sexual harassment. The basic principle is that the putative object of sexual desire gets to be in control. The object's control ideally should extend beyond how the other party acts to how he actually feels.

But it is not as simple as a toggle switch, notwithstanding the now-standard sexual rhetoric of turning on and turning off. Cold should ideally be a condition of sexual latency, rather than true asexuality. Even when a women or man wishes, indeed demands, to be treated coldly, she wants to be recognized as fundamentally attractive, should she wish and choose to activate it. Among the many types of glue that hold our fragmented world together, sexuality is one of the most important. It keeps the gaps between fragments from getting too big, while not eliminating them except, ideally at least, when sexual relations are consummated, which even under the best of circumstances occupies only a fraction of life. People talk, think, fret, and work on their sexual lives far more than they act on them.

Hot and cold, as poles of sexuality, are the basis of popular culture. A substantial part of mass media, perhaps the lion's share, is consumed with the hotness and occasional coldness of actors and actresses, models, singers, and socialites. This gives people something to talk about, and because of the slightly illegitimate nature of vicarious lust, is a ready way to forge weakly conspiratorial bonds with others. Media hotness has both obvious and not-so-obvious impacts on how ordinary people prioritize and constitute their own sexualities. Most obviously, people would like to resemble movie stars or models and are guided thereby in dress and promiscuity. Less obviously, people seem to care more about how they look to strangers, obliquely glimpsed and at a distance, than how they look on detailed inspection. Without this inversion of preferences it seems unlikely, for example, that the plastic surgery industry would have prospered. Hot acts readily and often best at a distance, and this is an essential part of its aptness for our world.

Another sense of hot and cold, in our times, polarizes the world between entities that are integrated with information and communication systems and technologies and those that are not. Hot is connected, wired, linked; cold is a kind of noumenon, a thing in itself. At first blush this polarity seems unrelated to the sexual one, but only until one realizes that people's sex lives are increasing lived online: ogling pictures of scantily clad gods and goddesses of the media, sharing risqué jokes, consuming pornography, exchanging sexually charged photos and messages with actual and would-be partners, constructing, twisting and masking identities to engage in fantasy or seek counterparties, and so on. Increasingly, like Kant's noumenon, cold things are in principle unknowable, deemed to exist in logic if not in meaningful experience.

Macrocosms

Thinking of Chinese geomancy and divination, or the common (though by no means exclusively) African notion that social disorder can cause natural disaster, Descola highlights correlations between micro and macrocosm in analogist societies. These correlations are quasi-solutions to problems of meaning and orientation in a fragmented world, a way to keep a bearing amid proliferating resemblances and hermeneutical possibilities.

Religion in recent decades has taken a decided turn toward micro and macrocosmic relations. Olivier Roy in *Globalized Islam* (2004) coined 'neofundamentalism' to describe the recent and powerful urge of many, whether Muslim, Christian, or Jewish, to seek a version of religion that is "pure" in the sense of removed from any particular social or cultural context. In Islamic neofundamentalism, for example, it is just the individual and sharia law. By aligning actions solely with sharia law individuals achieve a direct relationship with God. Roy associates neofundamentalism with globalization, which tautologically de-cultures events and actions. Paradoxically, neo-fundamentalists are very modern, and make avid use of the internet. Many of them mostly live online.

Environmentalism is a mainstream manifestation of the contemporary dynamics of micro and macrocosm, originating from the perceived downside of technological progress. Technological progress has had negative side-effects, with industrialization and urbanization transforming the natural landscape. Higher income levels and soaring population mean more consumption, depleting on natural resources and creating problems of refuse disposal. Discontent with civilization gives rise to efforts to reform it—in the more extreme formulations, before it collapses—while conjuring an anti-civilization of woods and wilderness.

This anti-civilization has acquired a global scope and focus, even as concrete experience of woods and wildernesses have receded in the lives of many. The shift in focus away from specific wild spots to the poles of planet and individual is captured in the environmentalist slogan "Think globally, act locally." As in the 16th century Chain of Being, the middle links individual and globe do exist, but are downplayed to avoid complexity and disorientation. The paradoxical result is an environmentalism that belongs to no place in particular and does away with the need for the ontological sameness in the physical world.

Preoccupation with genealogy

In analogist societies, Professor Descola notes

> an unparalleled proliferation of spatial coordinates and divisions of time: cardinal points, quarters, strict topographic segmentations, calendars, and—above all— long cycles of geneology. It is especially by means of these long-drawn-out lines of filiation that the great scheme of

intergenerational solidarities can be woven. It is a convenient way of justifying the permanence of groups of attributes and prerogatives that continue to be transmitted even with the passing of time; and it accounts both for the preponderance of place that ancestors frequently occupy in this mode of identification and also for the fearful reverence that surrounds them.

It is easy to see the proliferation of spatial coordinates in the marriage of internet technology with global positioning systems. Each of us can locate where we are to within a few feet and obtain a detailed map and directions to anywhere we might want to go, personalized to our particular needs, with a few taps on our smartphones. At a touch we can view our location, route or destination as an aerial photograph, or a street-level montage in which our fingers simulate our heads, swivelling the view left and right, ahead and behind to assimilate the full view and virtually orient ourselves. Similarly, we maintain calendars that allow us to reference arbitrarily long periods forward and backward at will, and prompt us with buzzes, pings and vibrations to the events we have set up in cyberspace, impinging into meatspace, as a semi-externalized controls that will only grow stronger as the old calendar functions are taken over by automated "personal assistants" that scan, organize and interact with our online selves and the linkages they entail using automated routines and artificial intelligence.

The importance of genealogy as a means of orientation and fount of enduring attributes and prerogatives in current society is easily underestimated, because the meaning of genealogy is being transformed in ways that make it consistent with the technological advance, general self-indulgence and material prosperity of the times, and because these transformations are still at an early stage.

Genealogy in the traditional sense may be least important. The internet era indeed has been a boon to genealogy, with specialized websites, online databases, and ready contacts and relations that in past eras would have required time, travel, expense, ingenuity and luck. Yet the present age shows no particular obsession with genealogy in the traditional sense. Most people would struggle to provide any details, say, about their great grandparents, much less regard them with fearful reverence.

The drawn-out lines of genealogy, though, are also represented in the growing importance of personalized genetics. For users, these services extract an orienting set of information from ancestry, reaching back far beyond even the most ambitious genealogical tree. There is rather more to this burgeoning field than the standardized processing of DNA to inventory individual traits and tendencies. A generous dollop of interpretation is involved, spurring debate as to whether doctors or internet entrepreneurs have the qualifications to provide it. The market is segmented. Some providers, for example, focus on health issues, while others offer a participative experience in leading-edge science. Purveyors tend to describe their service as "curation," involving taste, choice and values, and implicitly presuming a certain sophistication of the targeted audience.

The logical extension of personal genetics is selecting the genetic traits of offspring, beginning with gender. The lingering social importance of males and the drastic reduction in family size has already triggered a vast amount of crude selection, particularly in India and East Asia, primarily through abortion. Selecting the sex of the child at fertilization or shortly thereafter, along with the colour of hair and eyes, is an alternative that is only just starting to catch on. The possibilities for converting genes into a fungible consumer product, serving needs and strategies for relevance and power, are endless.

Sacrifice

Rounding out the psychology of disintegration, Descola finds it "impossible not to notice that sacrifice is present in regions dominated by analogical ontologies," surmising after Levi-Strauss, that the purpose of the sacrifice is to establish a link between initially unconnected terms, which of course is what analogy is all about.

As with genealogy, this characteristic poses an initial conundrum. The present era is indeed dominated by a discourse of victimhood and sacrifice. It furthermore has been overshadowed by the figure of the suicide-terrorist, a particular and deviant archetype of self-sacrifice with roots in the social fragmentation and cosmological proclivities of the era. The behaviours and beliefs associated with sacrifice in the traditional sense, though, are circumscribed to religious traditions, such as transubstantiation during communion for Christians, or the Hajj for Muslims.

The urge to sacrifice, Levi-Strauss' linkage of initially unconnected terms, explains the present moral tug of altruism. Google's Ngram, which tracks the frequency of word usage in books, shows that altruism took off in the decades after it was coined by Auguste Comte in 1851. It peaked in 1918 and entered a long decline. It was resurgent from 1960 to 1998, after which its incidence has plateaued. The first peak corresponds to its apogee under the naturalist ontology. It concerned the ordering of society with the sort of unifying laws that characterized the natural world, which was Comte's vision. Its latter renaissance is reflects the mental gymnastics of coping in a thoroughly fragmented world.

I wrestled with altruism as an undergraduate in the early 1980s, reading E. O. Wilson's *On Human Nature* (1978). The book popularized the argument that even complex human behaviours are genetically programmed, stemming from the imperative to transmit one's genes to the next generation. Altruism is dissonant within this paradigm, because it helps others' genes in lieu of one's own, and arguably ought to have been weeded out by evolutionary selection. Its popularity nowadays stands in tension with the deeply self-indulgent, consumable rootedness of personal genetics. But it is also complementary, in that both are ways of managing social entropy.

Apart from macrocosmic orientation, ethics has largely been reduced to consciously self-disinterested action, as opposed to, say, older ideas of codes of honour. Self-disinterest, though, is an illusion. Tautologically, I can only purposely do something if I want to, and if I want to do it I have an interest in doing it. This paradox merely internalizes the perennial dilemma of sacrifice. Sacrifice in olden days meant giving up something of value, the sheep, goat or whatever was offered to the gods. But it was also a way to influence them to do something good for you, or at least not to do something bad to you.

Thus altruism like virtual reality requires a fragmented notion of self and will, a 'real' self that is interested in doing the deed, and a 'virtual' self that sees the deed as contrary to what one wants. The real one is operative at the effective level and the virtual self conceptually.

Cybernetics of Practical Action

Getting things done in analogical societies entails procedures of integration, reliance on specialists in code and linkages of resemblance, recourse to roaming and possession, and a half-imagined worldwide collective in which divisions sustain the whole. All of these features also apply to our own contemporary society.

Mechanisms of integration

Maintaining a semblance of order in analogical societies, Descola finds, is a challenge:

> A world of singularities patched together from disparate materials in permanent circulation, constantly threatened with collapse on account of the bewildering plurality of its inhabitants, requires powerful mechanisms for pairing off, structuring, and classifying for it to become representable or, indeed, simply liveable for those who inhabit it. And it is here that analogy serves as a compensatory procedure of integration, making it possible to create chains of solidarity and links of continuity leading in every direction.

For one such mechanism, consider our reliance as consumers and individuals on a few key identifiers—particularly email addresses, mobile phone and credit card numbers, but also drivers' licenses and state-issued IDs—for structure, integration, solidarity and continuity. It is interesting, and in a way harrowing, to reflect that a little more than a century ago people went through life without them. Such identifiers either did not exist, or were limited to a tiny fraction of the population. Nowadays, remove them and it is you who ceases to exist.

The revolution in information and communications has galvanized the analogue of person and identifier. On the one hand, it has increased fragmentation and stressed the system by proliferating the creation and use of identifiers with limited domain and weaker power. People on average now have a few dozen online accounts with separate logins and passwords, which they cannot keep straight. They forget some and jeopardize others by making passwords obvious and repetitive. On the other hand, security specialists are pushing biometric authentication as a complement to, and eventual substitute for, old-fashioned passwords. Soon we will no longer have to remember whether it was our wife's or our son's birthday that we used in a particular case, nor what we did to thinly disguise it. Instead, the machine before us will automatically validate our face and fingerprint and let us in. The accretive fragmentation will once again be brought under control, and we will have come a small step closer to seeing our online accounts when we look in the mirror.

As another key example, consider the role of the International Organization for Standardization (ISO) in developing, producing, and distributing our welters of things. According to its webpage it produces 100 new standards per month, relying on 100,000 experts in 229 sub-committees. ISO's cumulative effort now runs to 20,500 international standards in all. It is, of course, only the most globally visible entity within a vast thicket of industrial, professional and regulatory bodies, public and private, national and international, that produce requirements with varying degrees of compulsion on how things ought to be done.

ISO's work is only partially successful. On the one hand, fast-moving technology is a source of disruption as well as progress. On the other, the world is still unable to agree even on basic measurement standards. Imperial inches, feet and yards jostle against the metric system. Specific industries have their own discrepancies of unit that often enough are a source of confusion and error, with natural gas, for example, variously measured in standard cubic feet or cubic meters, British thermal units or joules.

Code specialists

Descola finds across analogical societies

> a need to keep workable and efficient channels of communication open between all the parts of all beings and to maintain the many circumstances and influences that ensure their stability and proper functioning. The weight of these dependencies makes it essential to pay obsessive detail to a whole sheaf of prohibitions and prescriptions. So constraining are these that aid is usually required from specialists who are well versed in both the interpretation of signs and the correct execution of rituals and also in developing particular techniques for reading the future, such as astrology and divination. To find one's way through the forest of singularities, one needs a whole battery of symbols and emblems to make it possible to code all this diversity in a hermeneutic grid. To this end, semiautonomous systems for computing and combining, along with certain artefacts, many of which may be found in our

ethnographic museums, are pressed into service. They are used to clarify an overcomplex cosmos by plotting all its points of connection and major lines of force in manageable configurations.

His words need little elaboration or adjustment to match post-millennial civilization. Our prohibitions and regulations are legal and contractual (requiring lawyers, judges, arbitrators and law enforcement officials), regulatory (regulators and compliance officers), financial (accountants), technical (engineers), and systemic (systems architects and programmers). Such specialists are among the most highly trained, intelligent and well paid professionals around. Our techniques for reading the future are policy analysis, forecasting, and estimation, and our symbols and emblems are numbers and formulas, jargon and terminology. Our semiautonomous systems for computing and combining are ubiquitous.

Order through resemblance

Descola notes:

In the elusive world of analogism, resemblance becomes the only means of introducing order, for this is a priori a chaotic and inflated world, since it contains an infinite number of different things, each in a particular place and each at the heart of an idiosyncratic network. In order to reduce this dizzying atomist perspective, the links of similarity that justify repeatedly moving along certain meaningful paths need to be identified. Such links may be metaphorical if they present a similarity between terms, or metonymic if they concern a similarity in relations.

His elusive and chaotic world is a fine summary of that quintessential activity of our times, the internet search. The World Wide Web is indeed, to all intents and purposes, infinite. Google searches routinely bring matches numbering in the hundreds of thousands, millions, or tens of millions, and consequently people only concern themselves with the first few entries that searches return. The keywords entered for the search are an impromptu, idiosyncratic node, and the series of entries is really an inventory of other nodes to which it is somehow connected, ranked by presumptive descending affinity. I am at times a particularly dogged Googler, and have on occasion sorted through 15 or 20 e-pages. Even this persistence, though, is a drop in the bucket compared to the reams of virtual pages stacked invisibly beyond my screen.

It is an interesting aspect of the Google business model that a user's searches modify the search engine: the software uses artificial intelligence to "learn" from them searches what sorts of webs are likely to be more useful, and adjusts the results of future searches accordingly. Such learning delivers better results, to the extent that targeted and better are synonymous in the realm of information. It also helps Google buttress its lead in the search-engine market and achieve the sorts of response rates for advertising or "sponsored links" that make the firm lucrative. At the same time, though, it reinforces and heightens the atomism and idiosyncratic chaos that is the internet, and indeed the present reality. Google thus stands as perhaps the paradigmatic example of the glue that holds together the fragments of our civilization, with no pretension of fully eliminating the separation.

Roaming and possession

Descola notes that in societies with analogist ontology, beings are peripatetic:

> Given that every entity is made up of a multiplicity of components in an unstable equilibrium, their tendencies to roam are thereby facilitated. So the transmigration of souls, reincarnation, metempsychosis, and,

above all, possession all constitute unequivocal signs of analogical ontologies.

Possession, in the traditional meaning of the word, is lately on the rise. Pentecostalism, for example, went from 63 million adherents in 1970 to 631 million in 2014—almost a quarter of all Christians worldwide—and is projected to have 800 million followers by 2025. The defining event of Pentecostalism is the descent of the Holy Spirit on the followers of Jesus, manifested through spirit-gifts such as speaking in tongues and divine healing. Such beliefs and experiences are more than compatible with the present age. Most Pentecostals would likely argue that their faith is instrumental to successful adjustment to the modern world.

A 2009 Pew Research poll finds that in the US between a quarter and a third of the population believes in telepathy, communication with the dead and reincarnation. Some 15% believe in "channelling" or temporary possession by spirit-beings while in trance.

The persistence of belief in supernatural peripateticism, however vigorous, nonetheless pales before re-contextualization of such experiences in everyday life through communication and information technologies. A basic function of such technologies is to allow us to roam. When we project ourselves across space using media such as mobile phones or online videoconferencing, there is nothing supernatural about it; that is just the way things work.

We are all familiar with, though by now perhaps numb to, mundane possession of those around us. They sway, twitch, and sing to disembodied, esoteric bands, engage in animated arguments with Bluetooth interlocutors, or walk zombie-like staring into their display screens. The distant entities upon them are more vivid and immediate than physical circumstances, and the projection of their beings elsewhere is much more important, for the moment, than where they happen to be.

Some of the purest cases of transmigration and possession have to do with online identity. Most everyone realizes that identities now extend into the internet, where they can be readily manipulated, sometimes innocently and sometimes malevolently. Examples at the innocent end include creating an avatar for an online game or posting old or photoshopped pictures of oneself on Facebook. Less innocent is using a false identity, which in the internet era has its own specialized vocabulary (e.g., "catfish," "sock puppet"). At the far end is the quintessential modern crime of identity theft. It is hard to miss the parallels between the sorcerers of less technologically advanced analogical societies and the disembodied hijackers of self that lurk on the internet, waiting to trap the naïve or careless with relentless ploys. My spam filter usually catches a few suspicious emails per day; a few per week make it past the filter to my inbox.

According to a 2013 UN study on cybercrime, victimization rates varied between 1% and 17% of the online population for 21 countries surveyed, versus victimization rates for burglary, robbery and car theft below 5%. In a Pew Research survey from the same year, 21% of online adults in the US reported having an email or social media account hijacked and 11% the theft of information such as Social Security numbers, bank account data, or credit cards.

To the extent that our identity is not online, it is largely in things we have and experiences we buy and consume. Unsurprisingly, our "possessions" and transactions can turn the tables. We then undergo rites of exorcism in order to regain self-control. The model for the rites is mainly taken from retraining the body after traumatic injury or disease. Rehabilitation has thus spread from heart attack, stroke and car accident victims to alcohol and drug abusers, sexual transgressors, criminal offenders and the mentally ill of all stripes.

Rehabilitation nowadays may less often involve the overt banishing of evil spirits through religious invocation, but religious practitioners and specialists contest and share the space with medical, psychological and psychiatric professionals. There is an irresolvable debate as to whose methods and procedures are most effective, and when, in helping people overcome what are still routinely referred to as their demons.

The Sociocosmos

I have mentioned the polarization of globalization and selfhood in the particular, acute case of Islamic neo-fundamentalism, in which internet communications plays a vital enabling role. In a looser way, though, the internet is not just an enabler for a de-cultured, fundamentalist society to be envisioned and partially lived by its adherents. Rather, it *is* a de-cultured, global society in which all of us, to the extent that we live our lives online, belong. Each of us is a node in a World Wide Web that in principle embraces all humanity. The fact that the World Wide Web can accommodate something as specialized as neo-fundamentalism exemplifies the remarkable totalizing character of the general artefact. Descola again inadvertently describes the current situation:

> In an analogical ontology, the totality of existing beings is fragmented into so many examples and causes that the associations between all those singular units may follow

many kinds of paths. However diverse the morphology of humans and nonhumans recognized by analogism, those groups are nevertheless always presented as being constitutive units in a collective that is vaster by far, given that it is coextensive with the whole world. Here, the cosmos and society are equivalents, almost to the point of being indiscernible, whatever the various types of internal segmentation that such an extensive whole requires in order to remain operational.

In this "sociocosmic" society there is, for most, no particular moral agency or required order. It is merely the way in which we pursue the diverse ends of our lives, wills, and self. Yet it is, for many, instrumental to these ends, for hours a day, with the interfaces nearly extensions of our body. The neo-fundamentalist, who lives much more in the internet than in the particular, degraded society around him, is far from alone. In his guide to internet entrepreneurship, *How to Build a Billion Dollar Ap* (2014), George Berkowski cites a study in which a quarter of respondents worldwide said they share 'everything' or 'most things' online. India, Indonesia and Saudi Arabia, at the high end, are over 50%; in China it is a third.

The World Wide Web is operational ultimately because it is a polarized economic proposition. At one extreme, the hardware, operating systems, and basic service provide ubiquitous and permanent access, in principle to any other node, domain or page. At the other extreme, internet entrepreneurship relies on micro-segmentation, personalized marketing, and product tailoring as essential components of its business models and value propositions. Analytics capture and correlate the minutia of activity at the other end of the interface, generally through automated routines, tracking and sensing our preferences, foibles, desires and skills, and manipulating our environment in a way that caters to them. The global village of the internet is thus shattered into interconnected pieces.

III. PHYSICS AMID FRAGMENTATION

Physics has fully adjusted to the internet era: the fragmentation of society and nature; the reliance on computer and communications technology to furnish linkages, graduated interaction and direction; the psychology of disintegration and cybernetics of practical action. The adjustment is a tribute to the adaptability of the discipline that began, in its modern guise, in that fateful encounter of apple and scalp. But it is also the clincher for my argument. If even physics has embraced fragmented nature, then the old ontology of unified nature is well and truly past.

Fragmented physics

Stephen Benka argued in a 2006 editorial in *Physics Today* that if physics "were a person, it would suffer from a severe case of multiple-personality disorder:"

> Academic physics is fragmented into subdisciplines that sometimes feel a need to vie among themselves for some perceived legitimacy in the landscape of physics. Some have spun off into new disciplines, even new departments. So we find dedicated courses in, for example, acoustics or fluid dynamics or heat transfer are rarely available in physics departments today; interested students must look for them elsewhere... It's difficult to assess the state of non-academic physics... many who live there ply their trade invisibly; we don't know how to see them.

Benka divides physics into several main areas, none of which can be labelled without conjunctions: atomic and molecular physics; condensed matter and material physics; high-energy physics; nuclear radiation and plasma physics; and astronomy and astrophysics. He rejects what he thinks of as the popular dictionary definition that the essence of physics deals with "matter and energy and their interactions" as "trivial" and "self-limiting." What defines physics, he asserts, is rather that it has an "intricate array of tools" and a "precious mindset of rational exploration" that "deals comfortably with energy and matter of all kinds, and all kinds of interaction between them, in all kinds of environments." This is about as clear an expression of analogical ontology as one might expect to find: physical heterogeneity engaged through special tools by rare people combining extraordinary need for direct understanding with the ability and discipline to acquire the toolkit. The scripting imposed by tools and the broadest generalization of subject matter hold physics together.

The fracturing of physics into disciplines and subdisciplines is first and foremost a statement about the community of scientists who call themselves physicists, and it is clear that that community is suffering the stress of social entropy. But it also applies to the physical reality they study, inasmuch as the bifurcating and increasingly hermetic branches and twigs are an epistemological statement and fact.

Cyberphysics

In particle physics, for example, the medium for apprehension, organization, analysis and manipulation is the computer, and the implicit starting point is to redomain the physical world into cyberspace. Gian Francesco Giudice, a theoretical physicist at CERN, describes the prowess of the Large Hadron Collider (in "Big Science and the Large Hadron Collider," 2011) as follows:

> A new phase of proton collisions at high intensity began in March 2011 and on April 22, 2011, the LHC set a new record for proton-beam intensity (previously held by the Tevatron at Fermilab in Batavia, Illinois) at 4.6×10^{32} per square centimeter per second (equivalent to about 50 million collisions per second). A few weeks later, this value was almost doubled. The LHC detectors have performed stunningly, recording with staggering precision and efficiency the mountain of data coming from the collisions. At present, the LHC has entered the phase of direct exploration of phenomena never before studied.

But the scientists at CERN are not directly exploring the phenomena of 100 million sub-atomic particle collisions per second. They are instead studying the data after it is detected by instruments, translated into bits and bytes, and partially organized on computers. The celebrated experiments leading to the discovery of Higgs boson, for example, began by forcing bunches of protons to collide at a rate of one event every 50 nanoseconds. The raw data was initially screened down from some 20 million to 500 collisions per second, which still left around a billion events per year, or a petabyte of data. The computer system then applied over 200 algorithms to reconstruct the selected collisions "as accurately as possible" from the raw data, using the resources of some 6,000 computers.

Reconstruction relies on simulation models that were used to develop the algorithms to calibrate for imprecisions and malfunctions in the detectors. There are algorithms within algorithms allowing them to 'self-correct' in order to produce results from mountains of data, which are monitored semi-automatically for anomalies that could indicate a problem with the reconstructions. Massive numbers of simulations are required, roughly one for each real event. The full processing capability has a global network of 100 computing centers running batches of data.

The result of this effort is a kind of prospecting for particles, sifting through massive amounts of computerized reconstructions in search of novelty. The photons that are the raw material are natural, but created on demand within the LHC; the nebula of registrations from which fleeting results of photon collisions are frozen into data susceptible to processing and comparison are no one's property, and valuable to no one. The goal is to detect anomalies in the noise of ordinary reconstructions, disintegrations that indicate something new that can nonetheless can be accommodated within simulations and theory, and therefore be deemed an artefact of 'nature' and not a bug in the system.

The Cathedral, the Bazaar, and the Lab

In "The Software behind the Higgs Boson Discovery," (*IEEE Software*, 2012), David Rousseau gives the basics of the system at the heart of the LHC. Its programs use Linux open-source software, involving 1,000 user-developers initially, and the code evolves with some 25 changes per day. Upgrades are tested before release, but there is no formal code review. Major new releases including "significantly improved reconstruction algorithms, more accurate simulation to fix discrepancies observed with real data, and more accurate calibration constants" are released annually.

Reliance on open-source software is a response to issues of accountability and replicability that have become inherent to science in general, big and small, and physics in particular. Accountability and replication were straightforward when the experiment consisted, say, of rolling balls down inclines, as in Galileo's famous experiments on gravity. Gathering large amounts of data using highly specialized instruments, and manipulating and interpreting them with complex and often custom software and applications, are a different ballgame. Replication is much harder, and if the effort fails to yield the same results, it may be debatable whether the fault lies with the original effort or the emulation.

In the big science projects that the LHC epitomizes, accountability is diffused among a large, interdisciplinary group. None of the group's members fully understands or controls what the all others do, and therefore no one can fully respond for how it turns out or guarantee that it was done right (or fully define what 'right' might be). Given the amounts of dedicated resources involved and the evolution of the experimental and institutional apparatus over time, replication is out of the question. A unique project is on its own. In small science, conversely, the field of inquiry may be too narrow, the number of specialists engaged in the area too few to check each other.

Eric Raymond's celebrated 2000 essay on open-source software, *The Cathedral and the Bazaar*, asserts that traditional large systems are "built like cathedrals, carefully crafted by individual wizards or small bands of mages working in splendid isolation, with no beta to be released before its time." By contrast, "[t]he Linux community seemed to resemble a great babbling bazaar of differing agendas and approaches... out of which a coherent and stable system could seemingly emerge only by a succession of miracles." This is at heart a complex metaphor: the relationship of traditional major software projects to Linux, Raymond suggests, is the relationship of cathedral to bazaar. But Raymond was actually offering the image of the anarchic bazaar as a strawman of his own naïve, initial impression of open source software, which he partially demolishes over the course of the essay. The open source software approach doesn't work to create software, only to test, debug and improve. It requires a leader with people skills, who sets the community's norms, serves as a gatekeeper for ego-boosting that serves as the hacker community's primary motivation, and directs their selfishness toward cooperation to achieve the desired end. And it requires the infrastructure of the internet to cheaply access a sufficiently large pool of talent.

The main difference between cathedral and the bazaar approaches, Raymond argues, is that for the former bugs are deep and hard to root out while for the latter they are shallow and easy. This is strictly a large-numbers game: if enough people are scrutinizing the code, the problem will be obvious to some and the fix obvious to others. The open-source approach thus releases the software early, while it is still very flawed, and often: the whole point is to find the bugs and fixes. The contrast to the months of hard work by a dedicated few, who finally release a version that still does not work perfectly, could not be sharper.

The open-source approach also works because the software is modularized and debuggers are fragmented.

Many small groups work in parallel on sub-tasks, with little interface or interaction with the larger group, which is essentially defined and held together because everyone gets the code changes and bug reports.

The open-source approach to the massive software challenges of the LHC suggests a number of interesting identities. Scientists are hackers, with capabilities and credentials established through demonstrated contributions to finding and fixing bugs. Scientific leaders are non-coercive ego managers in the style of Linus Torvalds, the initiator and driving force behind Linux. Scientific disciples are the parallel pods of hackers working on subtasks. Scientific falsification is debugging, and scientific knowledge is the code. The broad measure of scientific success is an application that runs right. Nature is the real world where the effects of the application are felt.

Practitioners of open science will remain within large universities and research organizations. The more significant the problem, the more it will win grants and funding from governments through entities such as the National Science Foundation or, indeed, the Department of Defence. Progress will be supported and exploited by large for-profit players, and successes will generate fortunes through the intellectual property and spin-off businesses that are created. A 2015 CERN-led report (*Big*

Science: What's It Worth?) credited Big Science for everything from top drugs to scratch-resistant glass inter alia. The particle accelerator and related infrastructure at CERN got credit for the Hypertext Markup Language that enabled the WWW; touch screens; grid computing; the advanced detectors, accelerators, and magnets used in medical imaging and treatment; and big data capture, storage and analytics for banking, medical and other industries.

False science in the classic sense and bugs are not the same kind of error. To establish that an assertion about nature's laws, processes and conditions is untrue is not the same as saying that its codification and application do not provide the intended results. It has never been the case that science proceeds by blind trial and error, and all experimental systems and instruments of measurement are artefacts imposing intent. But building software and bug-spotting mean that we can recognize what we are looking for and know what it is. Thus they are already a step past the contestation of the basic suppositions and understandings. Producing results by conjoining cyberspace and meatspace is an exploration of a reality categorically different from even, e.g., the new vistas opened up by invention of the microscope. The possibility of replication is attenuated, and likely lost: it is absurd to think that the experiments of the LHC will be repeated. If divulged findings are later retracted, the responsibility for the inaccuracies may be more institutional than individual, and the retractions themselves may be merely 'upgrades' more than admissions.

Yet increasingly, these substitutes are the best that can be hoped for. If the reconstruction of the subject in cyberspace is the starting place for a scientific endeavour that then consists of analysing, controlling and manipulating it through computer programs, the programs obviously should generally run right. While it is asking too much that they be actually bug free, debugging through a regular process of review and improvement is the basis for reliability.

All this may be a particularly productive form of science, generating important discoveries for the foreseeable future. But it is something new under the sun.

Internet Physics sans Internet

The constrained fragmentation of nature does not rely on computers. Descola's definition of analogism in other, less technologically developed societies—i.e., the division of the world into a heterogeneous multiplicity with small distinctions on a graduated scale, recomposed into a dense network by analogical linkages, with resemblance giving the appearance of continuity and intelligibility—captures the leading edge of theoretical physics, string theory.

String theory holds that at the most basic level, the universe is made of 'strings', or extended objects moving in the four normal dimensions plus some six others that curve back on themselves almost immediately, like cylinders. There is no direct empirical evidence to support the theory, and no real prospects for getting any, largely because strings are too small to have any chance of detection even in the LHD. The theory is highly incomplete, owing in part to utterly formidable mathematics, also without any real prospect of a definitive statement. Some phenomena explained by other, more established theories have not yet been explained within string theory.

Despite these disadvantages, it has very successfully attracted theoretical physicists to work on it, generated top-cited papers, and influenced and legitimized work in particle physics and cosmology. Its influence now extends to the scientific method itself, with at least some advocates arguing for a relaxation of the principle of falsification as the bright line separating speculation from proven science. Such a move would, of course, obviously benefit string theory, but also be useful to the theory of the multiverse, which holds that arbitrarily large numbers of undetectable universes parallel to ours exist, and even inflationary cosmology, which like a black dress now goes with just about any empirical observation. String theory, for its advocates, would qualify as proven because of its elegance. This seems dubious grounds to other physicists, generating sharp rebuttals. A recent polemic in *Nature* led to a meeting of about 100 physicists and philosophers in Munich at the end of 2015 to debate the issue.

It is easy to see the naysayers' position. To make aesthetics, which is inherently slippery and subjective, the arbiter of realty is to make reality itself arbitrary, or at best to subject it to scientific consensus simply as a matter of taste combined with legacy institutional legitimacy. Once the legacy is rendered in these terms, however, the legitimacy thins quickly. Science has a track record of elegant wrongs, including notions that the universe centres on earth or the sun, light moves through aether, or species are invariant.

It is also easy to see the issue as a further example of the fragmentation of science and of physics in particular. The debate is evidence that fragmentation has progressed to the point that physicists as a whole can't even agree on what they are supposed to be doing, or how they will know if they've done it. Even this superficial assessment, though, moves the verification of scientific theory toward problems of community and consensus, the flip side of legitimacy. Thomas Kuhn pointed out decades ago in *The Structure of Scientific Revolutions* (1970) that new scientific theories do not pass the bright line test of falsifiability, but rather take over when the generation vested in the prior theory has died or retired. The challenge to falsifiability has emerged and strengthened in large part precisely because a new generation of theoretical physicists has come of age since the first major breakthrough in string theory occurred, in 1984. They are now in a position to take on the emeritus generation.

Richard Dawid, a philosopher-physicist who helped organize the Munich workshop, provides a more nuanced view of the implications of string theory's success for the confirmation of scientific theory in "Underdetermination and Theory Succession from the Perspective of String

Theory," published in July 2006 in *Philosophy of Science*. The first part of his argument is a kind of brush-clearing exercise, before consideration of the merits of string theory itself. Surely, he concedes, empirical falsification is the gold standard of proof, but it is a matter of degrees and not a single toggle that separates the proved from speculative. Notwithstanding Karl Popper's influential view of scientific advance as a process of hypothesis and falsification, that is not how theories are actually formed. Instead they emerge from the mind as proposed solutions to problems that physicists, based on their training, experience, insight, and indeed creativity, believe to be worth pursuing. Surely how the theory arises, and how it resonates, warrant some consideration in assessing its merits.

Dawid also points out shortcomings of empirical evidence. If a theory could in principle be tested through empirical falsification, but physicists cannot (yet) do so, then this is more a problem with empirical capabilities than a flaw in the theory. And even if a theory is consistent with all available empirical data, and sees some of its predictions confirmed through experiment, this does not mean that it is 'right'. Future data may emerge that contradicts it, or the parts of its predictions that could not be tested may turn out to be wrong, or (as with Newtonian physics) minor deviations from reality may be detected on finer measurement over more extreme ranges. Finally, there could always be other theories, as yet unconceived, that also fit all the data and pass the tests; theory is, in this sense, inherently and chronically 'underdetermined' by evidence.

These initial points deftly shift physics into the ontological priors of analogism. Empirical falsification is not, as used to be presumed, a testing of the dissimilar interiority of human explanation against the wholeness of Nature. It is testing fragments against fragments.

The rest of Dawid's argument, concerning string theory proper, in essence unpacks what string theorists mean when they (a) say that string theory is 'elegant' and (b) propose that this elegance is a kind of proof, standing in for empirical falsification, and compelling in its own right and way. Elegance effectively resolves into an assertion of the string theory's superiority as metaphor. The basic metaphor is that the most elementary particles are strings. In making this linkage string theory extends the standard model of particle physics, stretching its meaning without doing away with it, fulfilling without debunking it. A related assertion is that string theory is the standard particle model, the two intellectual enterprises, considered jointly, being a way of doing theoretical physics that gets well ahead of what empirical physics can validate. Though the standard model was formulated in the 1960s and 1970s, experimental verification of a key prediction, the existence of Higgs boson, tarried to 2012.

Elegance is also an assertion that string theory is valid because it is the best of all possible explanations, to the point that it has no serious contenders for what it mainly seeks to do, which is to account for gravity at the quantum level. This is an achievement that escaped the standard particle model. While the standard model holds sway, there is a rift between quantum and larger levels of phenomena. A unified explanation of the physical world has been a kind of Holy Grail for physics, and would serve as the ultimate confirmation of the fundamental ontological sameness of matter. String theorists feel uniquely qualified to provide the best metaphors of the fundamental unity of the universe, and to assess their superiority. Their metaphors are better because they are so mathematically rigorous and are based on such a detailed understanding of the world. They can tell what is productive and additive, or conversely limited and inferior.

The confidence of string theorists has grown over time, because the harder they work on their forbiddingly difficult and incomplete theory, the more they are convinced of its power. They have tried so many alternatives to string theory, including waiving, for the sake of argument, fundamental principles of physics, and found them deficient. This seems to put them rather in the position of Sir Arthur Conan Doyle's fictional Sherlock Holmes, asserting to Watson that once the impossible is eliminated, whatever remains, no matter how improbable, must be the truth. Furthermore, having concocted string theory to address quantum gravity, they have found that it addresses other particularly knotty conundrums in physics, e.g., supersymmetry and black hole entropy. What are the odds that it would do that if it were wrong?

Dawid suggests that string theory is not an aberration so much as a new paradigm for scientific proof. The bidirectional quality of metaphoric meaning comes through in this assertion: string theory is so strong because it so aptly embodies the new paradigm, and the new paradigm is viable because it is so aptly represented in string theory. Metaphoric circularity is logical circuity, if arguments must survive decomposition. It is ironic that string theory, which profiles as the last step in theoretic physics' millennial search for the most basic building blocks of the universe, should rationalize itself in holistic terms, as a kind of gestalt emerging from individual arguments, none of which, on its own, is sufficiently strong to make the case.

The unique qualities of string theory give some force to its proponents' claims of a paradigmatic evolution. It is the first theory in physics that does not require external calibration of constants in order to work. There is no equivalent to, say, the speed of light or Planck's constant, which are what they are because of the empirical evidence, not because theory dictates that they must have these values. In string theory, all that is needed is the mathematical structure of the string. That is still, of course, quite a lot, given ten-dimensional complexity that may ultimately prove intractable. But string theory nonetheless is uniquely self-contained. It is also the first theory that plausibly claims to cover the entire range of observed phenomenon, from the quantum to the cosmic, although it only does so by postulating another range of phenomenon that will elude observation at least for our lifetimes, if not forever. Finally—and critically given that the strings themselves cannot be observed—it exhibits scale invariance through a mathematical relation known as T-duality, having to do with the number of times the string is wrapped around a given cylindrical dimension. It means that the physics at the substring scale is effectively identical to those at larger scales. If string theory is true, physicists do not need to look deeper, as the risk of finding new data that would debunk string theory is nil.

The string theory challenge to falsifiability thus becomes a challenge to scientific progress itself. If string theory is accepted, the dialectical process of discovering new phenomena and devising new explanatory theories is replaced with a final explanation that covers all phenomena, down to the proverbial last turtle. The scientific enterprise thus shifts to fully understanding what it has got: developing and applying string theory notwithstanding its extraordinary mathematical complexity until its totalizing potential is realized. There is no reason to expect that the full maturation of string theory would occur anytime soon, if ever.

Dawid bills this as "a new phase of scientific progress," but it can also be seen as the rebirth of an idea with similar pretensions that died before ever reaching its full expression, the sixteenth-century notion of the chain of being. Like string theory, the chain of being held that all phenomena fit within an overarching theoretical schema of reflection and hierarchy, and like string theory, fully explaining the exact relations was a task for specialists, impossibly complex and never to be fully achieved within the minds of men. For the layman, with inferior intellectual resources and other preoccupations, it could be simplified into the correspondence of macro and microcosm, just as string theory's redefinition of the scientific endeavour would no doubt be headlined as the final linkage of subatomic and cosmic, but the metaphoric faith in macro/micro correspondence would be underpinned by the institutionally legitimized and perpetually unfinished explanation of all that lay between. With Dawid's new phase of scientific progress, in other words, we have the supposition of physical ontological fragmentation, in the form of an endless supply of phenomenon that can't be fully explained, interior ontological fragmentation, in the form of specialization within the bewildering panorama of unexplained bits, and the glue that keeps the fragments from spinning apart, in the form of partially elaborated but consensually authoritative string theory. For the time being, this thoroughly analogical ontology coexists with a further level of fragmentation, in its struggle for acceptance and contestation within the institutional community of physicists, as the old naturalist framework, which has been so productive for so long, fades.

IV. TRIANGULATING BY POWER POINT

I have worked in business for decades, but what working means has changed thoroughly. The essence of my first job, as a financial analyst in one of the international divisions of an erstwhile major oil company, was communication. I did not realize this when I took the job, but if I had I'd have thought I'd be good at communicating. My aptitudes and interests throughout my years of education were strongly tilted toward verbal endeavours. I was unprepared, however, for the communications I was expected to produce, and struggled to do them.

I had an inkling of unpreparedness almost the moment I walked in the door. "Now, C?" my new boss instructed me, "I don't like a lot of adjectives." If I recall correctly, he said this pre-emptively, before I had ever given him a draft communication for review. That was wise of him. I was eager to please and wanted to make a good impression, but even so part of me thought *but I like adjectives* while another thought *what does that have to do with finance?* and yet another *what difference can a few adjectives make?*

In the first thought, my choice of words parroted his. Couching it as a personal preference understated the issue for both of us. When he said, "I don't like a lot of adjectives," what he really meant was that adjectives were wrong and unacceptable. When I thought *but I like adjectives* what I really meant was that good writing had adjectives, to make it more vivid and interesting. But my desire to please and the power distance between us predominated, so I thought a second later *OK, so no adjectives.*

Months passed before I understood why he didn't like them. Only a certain type of communication was right. It had to be very clear, concise, and authoritative. Adjectives made the communications longer, and implied that the basic pairings of nouns and verbs were somehow deficient, standing in need of further qualification and elaboration. Adjectives smacked of subjective opinion and interpretation. They were shades of grey marring what had to be black and white.

The explicit part of each communication was only the tip of the iceberg. This is so with almost any overt communication, and if you don't get the submerged part right you are in trouble. The submerged bulk of the iceberg in this case was a composite of hierarchy, policy, history and specialization. The communications would be signed by my boss and go out under his name. hey carried the institutional weight of his position as an Assistant Treasurer and the division's financial authority, and the implicit weight of his boss, the company's

Treasurer. They almost always told someone to do something or approved or denied a request. The orders and sanctions were always couched as "recommendations," but compliance was obligatory, and any refusal was a challenge. The reason they were called recommendations was because the recipient did not work directly for my boss, so he could not give them orders without encroaching on the command of whoever was their boss. So the explicit sense of recommendations, whereby the recipient of the recommendation was in principle free to take or ignore the advice, was subverted to reinforce the company's hierarchy. To recommend was simultaneously to order and to evoke the dotted and solid lines of power in the division and corporate structure. When we really did mean to let the recipient choose whether or not to take our advice we called it a suggestion.

Almost everything was backed up by a policy, usually laid out in one of several manuals. I say "backed up," but that is not quite right. The policies were not some sort of foundation, or springboard, for our recommendations. Rather, our recommendations were the acts by which specific instances were created or appropriated by the policy, born or moved firmly and definitively under its dominion, and declared unexceptional. They did not just tell the recipient what to do, but also showed that the policy applied.

This was not done in a bureaucratic or heavy-handed way. We would not write, e.g., "you must apply Section 7, Paragraph 8 of the International Finance Manual." We would instead be at pains to explain why we made the recommendation, usually through a series of bullet points, which nonetheless had to be kept, with few exceptions, to a single page. The policy would be there, in the background, and our recommendation and its support would be consistent with the policy, drawing on its authority while simultaneously reinforcing that it was a good policy. The act of appropriating the specific instance under the policy largely consisted of enumerating the reasons, and when the recipient of the communication complied with the order he was also, implicitly, accepting that the reasons were not rebuttable.

We had thick and well-ordered paper files, and before drafting a communication would search through them for prior communications relevant to the case in consideration or similar past cases. This was, of course, a way to ensure that we were well informed in issuing and supporting the recommendations. It was also a way to ensure that we were consistent over time. The history contained in the files did not quite carry the weight that precedent normally bears in case law. But it nonetheless carried a lot of weight. The control it exercised on the framing of recommendations and the historical depth it brought gave our communications further authority.

The final component in this submerged composite was specialization. We were the Finance Department, and this is what we did. I was new, but my boss and most of the others had been thinking about and dealing with these same issues in similar ways for years or decades. It sounds as though I am talking about experience, but it is not quite the same thing. Rather, I am talking about the articulation of a specific domain of activity, Finance, from, say, Accounting, Tax, or Operations, and deploying resources and effort to maintain its distinctness as not just a feature of the company's topography of power, but a legitimate, necessary and good one.

You can readily see, I hope, how all four elements of the submerged composite reinforced each other and made the composite very strong.

Maintaining and building the submerged composite and ensuring every overt communication was attached to it was mostly how the vast and sprawling enterprise (some 70,000 employees deployed across most of the countries in the world) organized and coordinated its collective endeavours. The structure was necessary and sufficient.

It didn't need a lot of adjectives to prop it up. Adjectives were subversive of its hegemonic claim.

We had three secretaries in the department, and they were always busy, typing and retyping drafts, receiving and sending communications by telex or envelope, and maintaining the files. In contrast the department's two desk-top computers stood like cyphers under grey vinyl dust covers, in a marginal area along the main corridor leading to the Comptrollers Department. We had to get the Assistant Treasurer's permission if we wanted to use them. He was worried that people would play on them instead of doing their job. I remember using them for one assignment in the years I was there.

The system into which I had been so firmly inserted was, to use Descola's terms, quite naturalistic in its ontological conception. It presumed the fundamental uniformity in the physical world, whereby each event should be assimilated to a common framework, in much the same way that the items in a natural history museum fit into a common classificatory scheme. And it was about controlling the interior dissimilarity of the people who constituted the firm, to give the firm a transcendent consistency and coherence—an institutional weight.

I spent my days drafting memorandums, letters, and telexes by hand and revising the drafts until I could think of no possible way to improve them, then submitting them to the Assistant Treasurer for signature. For the first several months he would invariably redraft them— rewrite them, actually, usually within a few minutes from submission—and I would endure the minor humiliation of passing them back to the secretary (who had already gone through several drafts with me) for another redo. He was patient and courteous in these revisions, and the secretaries were more sympathetic than irked or derisive. I really was wracking my brain to be able to write at least a three-line telex that would not require comprehensive revision. Then one day he finally signed something on my first try: no comment or feedback beyond his neat signature in blue ink on the page. His secretary handed it back to me with a small comment and a sharp little look. I felt a minor sense of accomplishment mixed with disbelief. Was this a fluke? It was not. I had turned a corner in my training, and from that moment on more and more of my work passed muster, the number of redrafts until I was ready to submit a document declined, and I started to be used to represent the department in internal meetings and even business trips.

The structure of power I have described was not the only one in the company. I am sure, for example, that my experience would have been somewhat different had I been, say, a petroleum engineer or a geoscientist rather than an MBA type working in a support function. Alongside the official structures were some subversive ones, as well as a constant chaffing of egos against a system that valued consistency, conformity, and conservatism. But by and large the system worked everywhere and well. There was little sign that it was about to be overthrown.

À la recherche du temps perdu

The secretaries are gone, as are most paper files. Memorandums and letters have largely been replaced by emails, and nobody uses telexes any more. Desktop computers no longer stand largely idle, waiting for the boss to authorize their use; instead, if the computer is down, it is the worker who idles. Each of these changes is important in its own right, but peripheral to the main change that has taken place, simultaneously, in the character of business communication and the structure of corporate power. Workers like me no longer wrack their brains for the precise prose to appropriate a specific situation within the four-part submerged composite. Both the prose and the composite are gone.

The elements of the composite have suffered disparate fates. Hierarchy still exists, but in a truncated and compressed form, within a general context of greater informality and narrower power distances. There is little sense of a pyramid, but rather, quintessentially, collections of team leaders of varying permanence, interacting with decision makers who accumulate power and activity around them. The sense of history has dissipated, partly because few people stay with a job or company for very long; the mould of loyalty was smashed by all the down-sizing in the 90's and the economic crises of the new millennium. Even those who would prefer stability struggle for a career path within the attenuated hierarchies that persist. There is also a general feeling that history is no longer useful, or at least not nearly as useful as it was. Instead, the emphasis is on adapting to a dynamic and unstable environment that has the upper hand, or at least constantly threatens to seize the initiative. There is still specialization; indeed the tree of specialization has grown ever bushier as the division of labour has proceeded apace and the economy has become more complex. Specialists, however, tend to see themselves more as a floating pool of talent whose loyalty and ego are tied to other specialists in their group, for whom the particular company, collection of assets, and historical trajectory in which they exercise their talents is, at best, secondary. And vast new fields of specialization have emerged in informatics and communication, particularly around the internet, where there is little correlation between experience and mettle. Leading specialists can be only a decade out of school, still in the most rootless and transient time of life.

The domain of policy has also withered. This is partly a consequence of the diminishment of other materials in the composite (they all used to reinforce each other), but also reflects changes to policy itself. It is stuck in the middle: not flexible enough to meet changing situations and circumstances and assimilate the myriad of specifics it has to confront, and not detailed enough effectively guide behaviour. Nowadays, if policy is invoked (as in "this is a policy matter") it almost always means a) that there is a conflict and b) that whoever is trying to manage the conflict is seeking to resuscitate the old structures of power, whereby the particulars of person and situation could be subsumed within the hegemonic structure.

If all that had happened were the overthrow of the system that had been so robust when I began my professional life, business would be adrift, another victim, in its own way, of Fukuyama's Great Disruption. But instead other means to integrate have flourished, keeping the pieces together and gesturing toward larger meanings. Some of these means, such as standardization and proliferation of code specialists, have already been described in Part II. Such means, though important, are reactive and focus on control and constraint. The active principle in business comes instead from ways of communicating and envisioning the future that, if not completely absent in olden days, have hypertrophied in the new. They interact with the tools and practitioners of control and restraint, the one advancing, the other consolidating and thereby creating a platform for further advance. In this way the rhetoric and practices by which specifics were assimilated within a durable and hegemonic structure have given way to an ongoing colonization of an inchoate future.

PowerPoint corrupts

In 2003 Edward R. Tufte published a broadside against PowerPoint presentations entitled *The Cognitive Style of PowerPoint: Pitching Out Corrupts Within*. Coming from Tufte, the attack should be taken seriously. He is Professor Emeritus of Political Science, Statistics, and Computer Science at Yale University, and a renowned expert on information graphics. His webpage notes cite the *New York Times* describing him as the "Leonardo da Vinci of data," *Business Week* as the "Galileo of graphics." He is a man of conviction and determination, having once mortgaged his house to self-publish his now-classic book, *The Visual Display of Quantitative Information*.

If the attack is serious, so is the problem. The chosen mode for important communications in business is no longer, by and large, the memorandum or letter. Instead it is the slide pack. And the tool for crafting slides, under the hegemony of Microsoft, is PowerPoint.

The use of PowerPoint presentations as the primary mode of communication is not confined to business. The US military is famous for generating and consuming reams of slides, to the point where John Boyd, one of its most influential strategists, never captured his ideas in a traditional text, relying instead on several hundred slides entitled *Discourse on Winning and Losing*, the evolving basis for the briefings by which he achieved influence. Lawrence Freedman's *Strategy, A History* (2013) credits Boyd with setting the terms for the US military's exploitation of the revolution in information and communication technologies. PowerPoint is now used everywhere in government, higher education, and non-profit organizations ranging from international relief organizations to megachurches. If the cognitive style of PowerPoint corrupts, our brains are all rot, and all of our collective endeavours are blighted, from boardroom to battlefield and beyond.

While Tufte did not turn back the tide of slides, his was no lone voice crying in the wilderness. Louis Gerstner famously prohibited slide presentations at IBM. This move has been framed ever since, by Gerstner himself and others, as a key moment in his fabled turnaround of the giant, which when he took over in 1993 was dependent on an obsolete mainframe business and outmaneuvered by new competitors with rising technologies.

PowerPoint even addles rocket scientists. Richard Feynman, the Nobel prize-winning physicist, made no secret of his impatience with slide packs in his work on the Rogers Commission, created by President Reagan to investigate the 1986 Challenger disaster. Feynman recalled in a memoir, which Tufte quotes:

> Then we learned about 'bullets'—little black circles in front of phrases that were supposed to summarize things. There was one after another of these little goddam bullets in our briefing books and on slides.

NASA's corruption by PowerPoint merely spread with time. Tufte approvingly cites the criticism of PowerPoint slide packs by external investigation and oversight groups following the second space shuttle disaster in 2003. The Columbia Accident Investigation Board (CAIB) reported that a senior manager might easily misread the importance of a situation from a PowerPoint slide because key explanations and supporting information were filtered out, and found reliance on PowerPoint slide packs in lieu of technical papers illustrative of NASA's "problematic methods of technical communication." The Return to Flight Task Group continued criticism of NASA's overreliance on inadequate, disorganized, and unauditable PowerPoint slide packs that "tended to rely on mass, rather than accuracy, as proof of closure" of CAIB recommendations.

For Tufte, though, PowerPoint is not just sloppy. It is totalitarian, and the cognitive corruption it engenders is on par with that of the old Soviet empire. He opens his critique with a photograph of a 1956 military parade in Stalin Square in Budapest, which he adorns with comic-book style speech bubbles and thought clouds allusive to PowerPoint presentations. The giant statue of Stalin, for example, says "Next slide, please." The photo is followed by a quote from George Orwell's "Politics and the English Language" on the reciprocal nature of foolish thought and slovenly language. Tufte goes on to assert that "The PP cognitive style is familiar to readers of Orwell's remarkable and prescient novel *1984*," comparing bullet points to the thought-control nonsense "War is Peace," "Freedom is Slavery," and "Ignorance is Strength" from the novel.

PowerPoint's organization—"deep hierarchical structures, relentlessly sequential, nested, one-short-line-at-a-time"—and ethos—"advocacy not analysis, more style than substance, misdirection, slogan thinking, fast pace, branding, exaggerated claims, marketplace ethics"—reflect its maker, the large software corporation. This resemblance is not quite totalitarian, but the remaining gap is readily bridged: "Aggressive, stereotyped, over-managed presentations—the Great Leader up on the pedestal—are characteristic of hegemonic systems," setting up a "dominance relationship between speaker and audience" he notes.

Tufte analyses 217 model statistical graphics in 28 books on PowerPoint templates. They average 12 numbers each, vs. more than 1000 for *Science* magazine, 120 for *The New York Times*, and 32 for *The Economist*. This puts PowerPoint in the same league with *Pravda* in the Soviet-era, which averaged five. "Doing a bit better than *Pravda* is not good enough," Tufte observes.

It does even worse, "approaching dementia," in terms of density of characters. He analyses 189 PowerPoint reports, finding they average 250 characters per page and three per square inch, and 28 PowerPoint textbooks, averaging 98 characters per page and one per square inch. He compares them to the ten news sites on the internet including, in addition to the usual suspects, *People's Daily* of China and *Pravda*, presumably in its post-Soviet incarnation. The two average 4,100 characters per page and 43 per square inch. Thus PowerPoint is between one and two orders of magnitude less informative, and just above zero.

When he advises, as a near-concluding thought, that *"PowerPoint allows speakers to pretend that they are giving a real talk, and audiences to pretend that they are listening* [italics are his]" it is hard not to relate this to the old Soviet joke "They pretend to pay us, and we pretend to work." He closes his treatise with a repeat of the annotated Stalin Square photo. Beware of speakers using PowerPoint slides, who may be "serving up PP Phluff to mask their lousy content, just as this massive tendentious pedestal in Budapest once served up Stalin-cult propaganda to orderly followers feigning attention."

Critiquing the critique

One could pick a lot of bones with Tufte's critique. For example, is it fair or useful to compare PowerPoint slides to news sites (and other texts, up to and including the *Physician's Desk Reference*)? Many PowerPoint slides, after all, are shown while someone speaks. Is the appropriate character density what is written on the chart or what the presenter says? And is the number of characters per page really a good index of the value of a text? Many of his critiques seem focused on bad presentations and inappropriate use of PowerPoints rather than PowerPoint presentations per se. He devotes, for example, two pages to a spoof of Abraham Lincoln as a stumbling presenter using PowerPoint slides for the Gettysburg Address, treating it as paradigm instead of satire. The extended comparison to Stalinism, which serves as a guiding thread across the critique, is over the top. Bad presentations can be a boring waste of time or misleading, but are they really Stalinesque?

The main problem with Tufte's critique, though, is also its chief merit. He sees PowerPoint slide presentations exclusively within Descola's naturalist ontology of subjective fragmentation and whole nature, and there they really are inherently superfluous, mediocre, and corrosive. He therefore is blind to the inherently positive possibilities and value of PowerPoint slide packs within the double fragmentation of the internet era.

The cover photograph of the military parade at Stalin Square is a study in physical similarity: repeated squares of uniformed soldiers all facing the same direction and at attention, frozen in time. The mischievous, comic-book speech and thought bubbles reveal the interior cacophony. One of the senior officials says aloud, "Hierarchical order! Isn't it great?" as a soldier simultaneously asks, "Comrade, why are we having this meeting? The rate of information transfer is asymptotically approaching zero!" Meanwhile three others are variously enthusing internally, "For re-education campaigns, nothing is better than AutoContent Wizard!" "An integrated solution for show trials!" and "There's no bullet list like Stalin's bullet list" even as another thinks, "But why read aloud every slide?" and the giant statue itself drones on.

Tufte quotes Feynman immediately after Orwell. "For a successful technology, reality must take precedence over public relations," Feynman says, "for Nature cannot be fooled." Reality here means physical reality, and its monolithic continuity is reinforced by the singular, quasi-proper name, Nature, by which it goes. It could hardly be otherwise for Feynman as a 20th-century physicist.

Physical sameness is not menaced by PowerPoint; what is at issue instead is subjectivity, particularly the presenter's. Pitching without does not harm the without (for Nature can't be fooled), but rather corrupts within. This corruption occurs on many fronts. There is the corruption of excessive fragmentation, which comes from breaking everything into bullet points. This is not pith or condensation but rather foreshortening thought at the cost of coherence. Communication is reduced to listing, discourse to pre-sentences that are both syntactically and intellectually undisciplined. He quotes approvingly a *Harvard Business Review* article admonishing that bullet lists encourage laziness, are typically too generic, and skimp on logical relationships, at best presenting just one (e.g., priority). Such fragmentary listing is particularly bad, Tufte notes, at presenting cause and effect, with the former usually omitted entirely. Bullets are hopeless for complex cause-and-effect relationships.

There is the corruption of hierarchy. Each slide is arranged into its own mini-bureaucracy of bullets, often four to six levels deep, and each slide starts the bureaucracy afresh. This occurs regardless of whether the material at hand lends itself to strong hierarchy or division into one-slide increments. PowerPoint hierarchy thus serves as a kind of Procrustean bed for thought, its arbitrary form producing a choppy anti-narrative.

There is also corruption of barrenness. Slides are served à la Pravda, with just too little information to be of use. There is not enough to engage the reader or audience, which is not only boring but also anti-analytical, since the only way to really present data is to get it onto the same piece of paper in well-organized and well-presented detail, with honest and information-rich charts and graphics, and then pour over it. If it's not on the same piece of paper the mind doesn't pour, or thought at least becomes too viscous to do much good. Charts and graphics on PowerPoint presentations, in Tufte's experience, are neither honest nor information rich.

Then there is corruption of sequencing. Because the information on a page is so thin, it takes a lot of slides to get through the material. This exacerbates fragmentation and further interferes with serious analytical thought, because no one can remember clearly what was seven or fifteen slides back to compare it to what is on the current one. PowerPoint goes out of its way to engender this particular mind-rot, allowing presenters to use what Tufte calls "the dreaded slow reveal," whereby the presenter uses the software's animation features to unveil bullets on a slide one at a time, reading each one aloud before summoning the next, "on and on, as the stupefied audience impatiently awaits the end of the talk."

Finally, there is corruption of intent. PowerPoint almost inevitably leads to privileging of format over content. Slides are branded with corporate logos and loaded with pointless ornaments, some imposed by the particular templates that the organization requires its employees to use, others introduced at the presenter's whim. Presenters embrace their role of smirking salesmen marketing cheesy infomercials.

For all its verve and detail, Tuft's memorandum of grievances suffers at heart from a curious, almost inconsistent dichotomy. It is mostly the presenter, not the audience or reader, who is corrupted by all this. Others may be (must be) bored and are wasting their time. They may sit in good order and feign polite listening, but inside their minds are their own, with at least some remaining capable of both independent thought and critique, even among Stalin's soldiers. The dichotomy is despite the fact that most everyone in the audience is also a regular presenter, and thus exposed to the interior corruption of PowerPoint. Producers degrade; consumers are indifferent, cynical, frustrated or naïve, but ultimately immune. The dichotomy happens because the act of presenting moves it from the presenter's interior world, where dissimilarity is presumed, to the physical reality, which can't be fooled.

If delivered presentations are physical reality, though, it is a reality worse than just mediocre: it is dangerous and malign, because of the loss of discipline constraining interior fragmentation. This discipline is the essence of the bureaucratic proceedings of the international finance department where I worked in the '80s, of the discipline of natural history's totalizing and 'objective' classification schemes, and—paradigmatically—of scientific peer review on evidence-based work and replication of experiments. There is a direct line from its breakdown to the Challenger disaster, rocket ships burning up on re-entry. Tufte instead sees a Dark Ages spectre: our basic scientific and technological capabilities are at stake. The Soviet Union eventually collapsed; he implies that we may be headed the same way.

Tufte's critique nonetheless falls short, though, for in an era of double fragmentation, PowerPoint has come into its own.

Storyline coalitions

Of Tufte's criticisms, perhaps least fair is the charge that PowerPoint lets presenters be lazy. People like me who used to wrack their brains to write the perfect one-page memo (sans adjectives) now regularly wrack them to develop the perfect set of slides. This did not happen as a matter of convenience for presenters, or because PowerPoint's templates help presenters get over their nerves. The fact that what used to be called "visual aids" has hypertrophied and taken over the world of organized communication is due to something more profound. It is because the PowerPoint slide presentation is attuned to communication in our time. The suitability largely comes from the ambiguities it introduces, firstly in the relationship between sender and receiver and secondly between narrative and subject.

The presenter is presenting to an audience, and it is not quite clear who that audience is. Often enough, there is a single, powerful individual who dominates the primary intended audience. Even under these circumstances, though, there likely to be a nebula of other auditors in the primary group. There are an unspecified number of repeat performances of the presentation, which may or may not occur, with different audiences and almost always with the presenter not actually presenting, in which the material in the slides must largely stand on its own, helped along by the imaginative act of the virtual attendees as to what the presenter would have said had he done so. The uncertainty is compounded by the fact that the presenter is obviously performing as well as just sending a message—even when, as Tufte complains, the performance is bad and amateurish. Some performing is done as monologue or soliloquy, but some will be done by direct response to questions that may be raised, in orderly or disorderly fashion, by the audience, with the presenter lest he flop staying firmly in character throughout.

The situation is fundamentally theatre, and the sending and receiving of messages is like the communication between actor and audience. As theatre it is perishable, but its longevity and spoilage are unclear, in essential juxtaposition to a letter sent between two individuals and cc'd to other defined recipients, or a paper designed to withstand the test of time and be read and understood by anyone with the requisite training. It raises a series of fundamental questions as to the presenter. Is he giving the presentation or playing a role? Does he choose to play the role, or is it thrust upon him? While he is playing the role, is there another person who exists independent from the role, or is the role him? None of these questions has a clear answer. They may also exist with other forms of communication, but much less obtrusively.

PowerPoint presentations also introduce ambiguity between narrative and subject. The presenter goes through the sequence of slides, developing a storyline around the situation. When the presentation fails, it is usually because the storyline is absent or poorly developed, or rejected by the audience. The presentation is consequently about forging a relationship between the presenter and the audience as much as it is about the situation. This is in stark contrast, for example, to the old bureaucratic ways of proceeding, which were based on moments of positive identification between situation and policy, with a relationship defined a priori between sender and receiver.

A successful story-line simultaneously establishes a social order while offering unity and meaning to the situation at hand. Both the social and the situational order are ad hoc and perishable, and both are necessary. If they only last as long as the presentation itself, again the presentation fails. But even when they succeed, their ambition generally is to bridge interior and physical gaps only temporarily and imperfectly, in order to find a way forward in a situation that no one expects to grasp or resolve once and for all.

Storyline coalitions of relationship and meaning are fundamentally different from old political interest groups. In storyline coalitions interests can be inchoate, temporary, and even inconsistent. They exist when the audience buys into the narrative with which the presenter (in his role) unifies and gives meaning to the subject matter. The language of purchase and investment invoked in the oft-used term "buying in" is not accidental. It is a pragmatic and transactional acquiescence using a fungible medium, appealing to valuation on balance rather than whole-hearted agreement. Both presenter and audience might adopt an inconsistent or even contradictory storyline in a different presentation.

Like role playing, storylines are not unique to PowerPoint presentations. The phrase has been adopted from drama and fiction, novels, theatre or movies. But in PowerPoint presentations, storylines move from entertainment and art to purposeful and organized activity in business, government, the military and so on. Unifying interpretations are hybrids, partly creative and partly logical. This is infuriating to Tufte, for whom the storyline is merely a pitch, the presenter who uses them a huckster. But they may be as good as one can hope for nowadays.

Storylines are unremarkable and do not vary so much. Most can be boiled down to just two basic types: either the organization is faced with an opportunity and should seize it (thereby advancing toward achievement of its overarching goals) or it is faced with a threat and should take action to neutralize or avoid it. Either one presumes a unity of purpose and a degree of control over events that could be readily challenged.

The overarching characteristics of PowerPoint presentations—theatre and roleplaying, ambiguity of relations and storylines—are embodied in individual slides. Tufte's bugaboo, fragmented bullet points pushed into an overly hierarchical framework with any accompanying charts only fluff, branding, or at best a few meaningful numbers, is real enough, but represents only one end of a continuum. At the other end of the continuum are slides with charts or tables but few or no words beyond the title of the slide. The presenter generally includes these slides because the information presented in a chart or figure is so complex or dense that it needs a lot of space to be seen and digested. The presenter may also want to juxtapose several charts at once, leaving little space for text. On such occasions the charts may have enough expressive power on their own, or be obvious enough, that bullets are judged superfluous, or alternatively the bullets may be provided on the following slide as a practical matter. Alternatively, the charts may have been included not for purposes of the presentation itself (the presenter merely showing they are there and mentioning their contents) but rather as back-up support, which those who are so inclined can peruse and consult after the presentation is done, or beforehand if the slides are distributed in advance. Such charts and tables are what Tufte would like presentations to be about, with everyone digging into the data and contesting analyses, and this activity is indeed possible. But the focus instead is the storyline coalition.

The most interesting slides, however, are midway across the continuum, with a balance of bullets usually taking up the left half of the slide, one or two substantive charts or figures on the right, and a synergy between the two halves, with each one adding something to the other. PowerPoint works to produce these sorts of slides, and good presentations rely mostly on them.

Chart semiotics

The basic structure of a balanced slide, chart on the right and bullet on the left, juxtaposes two predominant kinds of meaning, semiotic and semantic. This structure gives it metaphoric depth and complexity. The semiotic meaning predominates in the charts and figures on the right, but the right-hand side also has semantic meaning in the chart title, axes, legends, labels and so on. The semantic meaning predominates in the bullets on the left, but as discussed later, the bullet panel carries a secondary semiotic value.

The material filling the right of the slide may be diagrams, photographs, maps, or graphs, the usual types of graphs being bars, lines, or pies. These are meant to represent some aspect of the dilemma, analysis or solution pursued in the storyline. The audience is meant to experience a faint shock when it sees them, whether of imagination (when it triggers visualization), coherence (when it imposes order, sequence and hierarchy), orientation (when it locates and directs), or recognition (when it sees relationships and patterns). These minor shocks may be pleasant or unpleasant, with the tension usually generated earlier on in the story and the resolution later, but they should forge a bond with the presenter. They are literally what the presenter presents to the audience, the rest being discussion around it. It is thanks to the semiotic power of the charts and figures that the presentation transcends the bland, even sterile surroundings of the meeting or briefing room to jointly confront, albeit in purely symbolic terms, the world outside. But they are not really the external world: they are instead carefully selected, contrived, synthetic and distorted simulacra thereof, in each sign individually and also in the order in which they are presented. If the presentation is the least bit artful, the signs will be furthermore assimilated into a formal order of standardized font size and type, colour scheme, and so on. This order is meant to be aesthetically pleasing, temporarily narrowing the fragmentation through purely stylistic control and uniformity.

The storyline is often characterized as "data-driven", which is meant to communicate both that the presentation has substance and that the presenter's subjectivity has been disciplined. But the data generally is not examined or validated within the presentation, beyond citing the source. An organization needs a separate process of vetting and quality control for that, and if it has not occurred by the time the presentation is made there is a problem, although the problem is not in the presentation per se. When it does occur during the presentation, it usually means that the presentation has broken down and failed.

A good example of PowerPoint semiotics (from my own background) is seismic interpretation in presentations on hydrocarbons exploration. Seismic surveys for oil and gas exploration involve gathering petabytes of data in intensive acquisition campaigns that use sophisticated sensors to measure and record the echoes of shock waves traveling through layers of sedimentary rock and ancient, buried reefs. This data is gathered over square miles of distance and thousands of feet below the surface of the earth or seabed. It is processed using specialized software run on powerful computer workstations. The most common output from this effort is a stylized image of a specific cross-section of the earth's crust, extending a mile deep or more. It is a computer image, of course, and not a picture of the real thing. Before it is inserted into the presentation slide it is routinely distorted via colour coding (usually bright colours) and exaggeration of the vertical relative to the horizontal, so that subtle arcs and dips seem obvious and significant even to unpracticed eyes. The purpose is to draw attention to subterranean structures where oil and gas may be trapped.

The image in the slide is then incorporated into the storyline. The general exploration storyline is that committing further time, effort and money to evaluating the structure is an opportunity for the firm to achieve its overriding goals of profitably discovering, developing, producing and selling hydrocarbons volumes. The specific storyline is usually wonderfully colourful, involving heaving tectonic plates, vanished oceans and rivers, vast climate swings, fossil remnants of extinct species, and high-stakes gambles for buried treasure.

It is important to remember that the data is never completely real. If it is historical data, it was precipitated from the world using measurement tools and then further processed and manipulated. If it is counterfactual data—a forecast or a proposal for something that does not exist— then it was likely produced through, or indeed is itself, a model, or a model of a model. It is also forced into a two-dimensional space where pattern recognition and comparison can be readily made. Data and model outputs focus on producing such spaces because of this pragmatic utility. But that is not the same thing as saying that the models can be reduced to the outputs.

Contrary to Tufte, such a focus does not mean that the underlying analysis is forced into simple modes of causality in the models, the presentation, or the minds of speaker or audience. Multivariable regression models, for example, employ statistical techniques to estimate the influence which a measured (quantified) series of causes—i.e., independent variables—exerts over a measured, quantified effect—the dependent variable—over time or across instances. Each independent variable is a separate dimension, but what is graphed is usually just the history match, showing the actual measured and quantified data for the dependent variable against the model's estimate for that same data using the formula generated for the independent variables. Anyone can see how close the model estimates comes overall to the "actual" historical data, where it is closest and where it diverges the most.   Other models can incorporate feedback loops, bidirectional causality, and so on.

Modelling loosely fills the role that policy used to, but of course they are fundamentally different. Models are not aimed at capturing reality and constraining action within synchronic rules, but seek to project the future and test alternatives, knowing full well that the forecasts have a probability of actually occurring, exactly as shown, that approaches zero and variations and revisions—perhaps extensive or radical—to what is presented will have to be contrived into existence as the situation evolves.

Our contemporary fixation on data, models and presentations is another instance of our characteristic preoccupation with the interrelations of macro and microcosm. Assessing distant, kindred societies, Descola observes:

The obsession with correspondences between humans and the cosmos made it possible to establish one privileged creature as the seat of a denser focus of such correspondences, which checked both the proliferation of signs at that level and also their limitless reverberation within a closed world. This seemed to guarantee that an ordered system of knowledge and a restorative practice were possible, that in the unremitting flood of similarities, a guiding map was available.

As with past analogical societies, PowerPoint presentations make guiding maps available, providing some order and control within a flood of reverberating signs and similarities that threatens to overwhelm. While the signs in PowerPoint usually are not detected in the human body itself—in the way that, for example, Plato's *Republic* proposes a correspondence between man and state so close that it is not quite clear which it is really concerned with—they are always used to confer a central role to a small group of humans—the presenter and his audience—whose will and actions will then be projected out on the broader world, remaking it in their own image.

It is no coincidence that the rise of PowerPoint presentations coincides with the rise of globalism. As an undergraduate I had an interdisciplinary major called "International Economics and Cultural Affairs" and went on immediately to take a master degree in International Business Studies before working in the Latin America/West Africa Division of a major oil company. In all three cases the epistemological and organizational order envisaged the world as motley countries and cultures where one could only function effectively through a combination of specific local knowledge and tools of orientation and appropriation. This order was uprooted as internationalism gave way to globalism, in which the basic vision is that protagonism and dependency are played out on an earth-scale. While not quite cosmic in scope, the global scale carries an inherent threat of disorientation and disempowerment.

The basic schemes of navigation in a world of fragmented being are as captured in the diagram on the following page. The operant rule is if the semiotic outcomes from simulated alternatives and futures in the well-constructed, artificial microcosms of models are sufficiently good and robust, commitment at the macrocosmic level is warranted, even required. This rule is, of course, integrated into the overall storyline and associated storyline coalition between presenter and audience. The feedback loop from semiotics back to macrocosm is nothing new, although our era's towering technology may mean that the storyline coalition sometimes has a higher degree of influence on the macrocosm than has historically been the norm in societies with similar ontological priors.

Figure 2: Microcosm/macrocosm dynamics in PowerPoint presentations

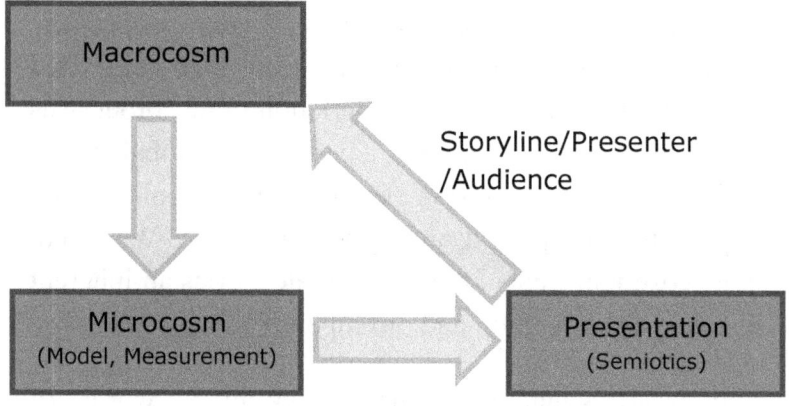

Bullet exegesis

The left-hand side of the chart, in such prototypically balanced and interesting slides, conveys primarily semantic meanings. The meanings are fundamentally about the sign to the right and how it relates to the macrocosm. It thus expresses the meaning of the sign, but in a compressed and hierarchical language of bullets.

This peculiar language of bullets accomplishes several things. Rather superficially, it allows the slide to use a larger font size, which makes the words intelligible to a larger and more physically distant audience, thus performing a function of inclusion and extension. It also shifts the relationship between the individual bullets from language itself to the visual hierarchy. This allows them to be ordered through classification and subordination but leaves other relations, as Tufte complained, often unspecified. The speaker who presents the slides must fill in the blanks. The bullet panel thus is a polyvalent visual symbol of its own: it symbolizes the presenter's perishable discourse, the audience's comprehension, and the stilted and stunted nature of relations.

Paradigmatically, the bullet panel will contain two main bullets, each with two to four subordinate points. The first main bullet articulates and reinforces the interpretation that the audience should have glimpsed on its own from looking at the symbol on the right. The second extends that meaning, showing that the presenter has gone beyond the audience in grasping the meaning of the sign, surprising them with new insight. Both the confirmation and the new insight reward the audience and breathe life into the fleeting storyline coalition.

This arrangement, not accidentally, has parallels to the sort of Bible study I grew up with, as a Methodist in a small town in the Midwestern United States. The charts, mostly though not entirely symbols, are like the verses taken from the sacred book and deployed for consideration. The bullets, profane in comparison, are the commentary on it, which mix the obvious with the erudite, reinforcement with depth. The presenter above all resembles a minister preaching a secular, perishable religion to an ad hoc congregation.

The title across the top of the chart, of course, captures the union of the two halves below while reinforcing the linkage between the slide's specific contents and the overall storyline.

Signs to strategies

Good presentations are hard to do, so it is not surprising that many are mediocre. But when the presenter and presentation are good, they succeed in building a bridge from the visual outputs of the microcosm to strategy, purposeful and coordinated action to align the macrocosm with desires and goals. The bridge between the two is rhetoric, a forgotten and neglected skill in the era of naturalist ontology, but back with a vengeance now.

Successful rhetoric combines both logical argumentation and emotion, our search for understanding and power together with our search for community, prestige, and security. It is primarily hermeneutical, as the presenter imposes his interpretation on the audience and then leads them to act on it.

Just as the rise of PowerPoint presentations corresponds with the rise of globalism, it is also linked, again by no mere coincidence, to strategy. In the current milieu strategy is ubiquitous, but also, rather ironically, under constant threat of trivialization and futility. Lawrence Freedman opens his monumental history of strategy with a quote from prize fighter Mike Tyson—"Everyone has a plan 'till they get punched in the mouth"—that suggests that strategy as a concept is fragile to the point of meaninglessness. He follows with the suggestion that strategy as a word has been voided from overuse:

> Everyone needs a strategy. Leaders of armies, major corporations, and political parties have long been expected to have strategies, but now no serious organization could imagine being without one... Strategies are now offered not only for the life-or-death, make-or-break decisions of great states and large corporations but also for more mundane matters. There is a call for a strategy every time the path to a given destination is not straightforward or whenever judgments are required on resources needed, their effective application, and their appropriate sequence... In fact, there is now no human activity so lowly, banal or intimate that it can reasonably be deprived of a strategy.... Can the same word apply to battle plans, political campaigning, and business deals—not to mention coping with the stresses of everyday life—without becoming meaningless?

The sprawling text goes on to discuss strategy's origins in human evolution and ancient texts from the Bible, proceeds through Sun Tzu and Machiavelli to (rather surprisingly) Milton's *Paradise Lost*, and then explores in turn military strategy, leftist and activist "strategy from below", and business strategy. Some 600 pages later, by way of summing up, the best he can do is to advance the notion that strategies are forward-looking scripts, that is, story-lines that tell those concerned what they ought to do. They have more in common with movies dramas (Freedman particularly likes *Mr Smith Goes to Washington*) than science, the main exceptions being that in strategies "the stakes are for real," that strategies are more messy and uncertain than movies, and that in strategies the outcomes are uncertain and lacking closure, with the strategist always aiming for comedy (i.e., a happy ending) but risking tragedy (a sad one, at least for the protagonist).

Though his thoughts are presumably about as far as can be from PowerPoint presentations, Descola unwittingly offers an alternative definition of strategy that may be at least as good:

> Analogy is a hermeneutic dream of plenitude that arises out of a sense of dissatisfaction. Noting that the general segmentation of the world's components is based on a scale of small differences, it nurtures the hope of weaving these slightly heterogeneous elements into a web of meaningful affinities

and attractions that gives the appearance of constituting a continuity.

PowerPoint presentations are efforts to navigate in the uncertain, fragmented shiftiness of our analogical times. Notwithstanding Tufte's foreboding, they seem unlikely to be the cause of our society's eventual collapse. The rhetoric of PowerPoint is not just a matter of losing the methods and capabilities of naturalist ontology. It is also a matter of positive adaptation to the new good and bad.

CONCLUSION

I took the liberty of not revealing until middle of the book that Descola's foray into comparative ontological anthropology, and the rather eerie applicability of the characteristics of analogist societies to our own, launched my train of thought. Instead I began inductively: if we look, walk, and quack like ducks, then ducks we must be.

I also have taken a liberty by shying away, until now, from an implication of the cracking of the physical monolith that has pended since "No One Knows," my first chapter on the internet's implacable nudging. That implication is the demise of the mind-body dualism that was a staple of the pre-internet era. Even during the naturalist era, a lot of work had been done to undermine the idea of an independent mind, in neurology, evolution, and even artificial intelligence. Yet the underlying presumption was still the idea of fundamentally heterogeneous subjectivities approaching a fundamentally continuous physical world, with a hard distinction at a basic ontological level between them.

The outstanding fact of the internet age is not that the individual subjectivities have ended, but rather that the presumptive continuity of the physical world has ended, and the hard ontological distinction between mind and outside world beyond has become grey. Mind and body have become alike in their fragmentation, and as they have done so the emphasis has shifted, from using the former to plumb the latter, to holding the bits of both in check. The old, naturalist era was at heart about exploration, while the new, analogist era is forever swimming against the tide of entropy.

The arc of modern ontological history is as follows. Modern mind/body dualism dates to Newtonian discoveries of unity of phenomenon (physical law) and continuity of change (calculus). Exploration of the world scientifically and literally (these areas of endeavour overlapped) drove material progress and technology while underscoring the subjective heterogeneity of humankind. Technological and material advances led to increasing subjective fragmentation at an individual level, to the point of threatening social disintegration in society as a whole, and disciplinary disintegration within science. Information technology has helped to curb without eliminating subjective fragmentation, but also broke down the monolith of physical world through a confluence of factors. These include the rise of a virtual space where effective action occurs; the ambiguity of physical identities with online linkages stepping into the gap, to the point where it is no longer clear that the people we deal with are people at all; the drift of self, organization and direction across the interface to cyberspace; and the empowerment of the parts of the population, and the aspects of the mind, that are predisposed to experience the world in fragments.

Science itself adapts to the new reality, in ways so fundamental – Dawid shows – as to put paid to the notion of scientific proof itself, relying instead, and thus taking into its essence, what can only be described as one of the most stunningly sophisticated analogist orientations ever created by man. But it is not the same science as before. There is rather more than a paradigm shift, in the Kuhnian sense, at work here. The paradigm for paradigms has shifted.

Dilemmas of orientation and effective action overshadow this doubly fragmented world. The effort to manage the dilemmas has led to an almost ubiquitous nexus of PowerPoint presentations and strategy as a rhetoric of purposeful action. Perhaps I should have developed these essays as a slide pack. But I'm just trying to say what we are, not what we should do.

Bibliography

Ahuja, Anjana. "Autism Makes a Happier Silicon Valley." *FT Wealth* (May 16, 2014). Accessed May 29, 2016. http://www.ft.com/intl/cms/s/2/349d3872d96f11e3837f00144feabdc0.html.

Autistic Spectrum Disorder Fact Sheets. Computers in Sensory Integration. Accessed May 19, 2016. http://www.autismhelp.org/interventionsensoryintegrationcomputers.htm.

Badger, Emily. "Millennials Say They'd Give Up Their Cars Before Their Computers or Cell Phones." *The Atlantic Citilab* (February 28, 2013). Accessed May 14, 2016. http://www.citylab.com/commute/2013/02/millennials-say-theyd-give-their-cars-their-computers-or-cell-phones/4841/.

Benka, Stephen G. "The entangled dance of physics." *Physics Today* (December 2006). Accessed June 27, 2016. http://scitation.aip.org/content/aip/magazine/physicstoday/article/59/12/10.1063/1.2435682.

Berkowski, George. *How to Build a Billion Dollar App*. London: Piatkus, 2014.

Big Science: What's It Worth? Science|Business Publishing Ltd, 2015. Accessed July 13, 2016. http://www.sciencebusiness.net/eventsarchive/OpenScience/BigScience.pdf.

Brown, Eileen. "Phone sex: Using our smartphones from the shower to the sack." *ZDNet* (July 11, 2013). Accessed May 6, 2016. http://www.zdnet.com/article/phone-sex-using-our-smartphones-from-the-shower-to-the-sack/.

Carr, Nicholas. "Is Google Making Us Stupid?" *The Atlantic* (July/August 2008). Accessed May 29, 2016. http://www.theatlantic.com/magazine/archive/2008/07/is-google-making-us-stupid/306868/.

Carr, Nicholas. "The Web Shatters Focus, Rewires Brains." *Wired* (May 24, 2010). Accessed May 25, 2015. http://www.wired.com/2010/05/ff_nicholas_carr/.

Casadevall, Arturo and Ferric C. Fang. "Specialized Science." *Infection and Immunology* 82:4 (April 2014), 1355–1360. Accessed June 19, 2016. http://iai.asm.org/content/82/4/1355.full.

Castells, Manuel. *The Power of Identity: The Information Age: Economy, Society, and Culture Volume II.* New York: Wiley-Blackwell, 2009, Second Edition.

Centers for Disease Control and Prevention. Autism Spectral Disorder (ASD) Data and Statistics. Accessed June 4, 2016. http://www.cdc.gov/ncbddd/autism/data.html.

Coleman, Gabriella. *Hacker, Hoaxer, Whistleblower, Spy, The Many Faces of Anonymous* (London: Verso, 2014).

Cone, Maria. "Autism Clusters Found in California's Major Cities." *Scientific American* (January 6, 2010). Accessed May 29, 2016. http://www.scientificamerican.com/article/autismclusterscaliforniahighlyeducatedparents/.

Cortez, Marc. "The Growth of Global Pentecostalism (Wheaton Theology Conference 4)." Everyday Theology, April 16, 2014. Accessed November 4, 2015. http://marccortez.com/2014/04/16/growth-global-pentecostalism-wheaton-theology-conference-4/.

Csikszentmihalyi, Mihaly. *Flow: The Psychology of Optimal Experience* (New York: Harper & Row, 1990).

Davis, Lennard J. *Obsession: A History.* Chicago: The University of Chicago Press 2008.

Dawid, Richard. "Underdetermination and Theory Succession from the Perspective of String Theory." *Philosophy of Science* 73:3 (July 2006). Accessed July 23, 2016. http://homepage.univie.ac.at/richard.dawid/Eigene%20Texte/12.pdf.

Descola, Philippe. *Beyond Nature and Culture*. Chicago: The University of Chicago Press, 2013.

Diamond, Jared. *Collapse, How Societies Choose to Fail or Succeed*. New York: Viking Penguin, 2005.

Douglas, Mary. *Purity and Danger, An Analysis of Concept of Pollution and Taboo*. New York: Routledge Classics, 2002.

Ellis, George, and Joe Silk. "Defend the integrity of physics." *Nature* 516:18 (December 25, 2014). Accessed June 20, 2016. http://www.nature.com/news/scientific-method-defend-the-integrity-of-physics-1.16535.

Fattouh, Bassam. *An Anatomy of the Crude Oil Pricing System*. Oxford: The Oxford Institute for Energy Studies, January 2011. Accessed September 11, 2015. https://www.oxfordenergy.org/wpcms/wp-content/uploads/2011/03/WPM40-AnAnatomyoftheCrudeOilPricingSystem-BassamFattouh-2011.pdf.

Fliesler, Nancy. "Autism and Asperger's Are Different…at Least on EEG." Vector. August 15, 2013. Accessed May 19, 2016. https://vector.childrenshospital.org/2013/08/autism-and-aspergers-are-different-at-least-on-eeg/.

Florida, Richard. "Why Young Americans Are Driving So Much Less Than Their Parents." *The Atlantic Citilab* (April 10, 2012). Accessed May 14, 2016. http://www.citylab.com/commute/2012/04/why-young-americans-are-driving-so-much-less-their-parents/1712/.

Floridi, Luciano. *A look into the future impact of ICT on our lives*. September 1, 2006. Accessed April 24, 2016. http://www.philosophyofinformation.net/wp-content/uploads/sites/67/2014/05/alitfioiool.pdf.

Floridi, Luciano. "The Informational Nature of Personal Identity." *Minds & Machines* 21 (2011), 549-566. Accessed April 30, 2016. https://pdfs.semanticscholar.org/ac0e/bf3fff00cfd5763e3e249df2693592812ddd.pdf.

Foucault, Michel. *Madness and Civilization: A History of Insanity in the Age of Reason.* New York: Random House, 1965.

Foucault, Michel. *The Order of Things: An Archaeology of the Human Sciences.* London: Routledge Classics, 2002.

Freedman, Lawrence. *Strategy, A History.* New York: Oxford University Press, 2013.

Fukuyama, Francis. *The Great Disruption, Human Nature and the Reconstitution of Social Order.* London: Profile Books, 1999.

Gallup. "Confidence in Institutions." Accessed October 7, 2015. http://www.gallup.com/poll/1597/confidence-institutions.aspx.

Giudice, Gian Francesco. "Big Science and the Large Hadron Collider," CERN-PH-TH/2011-288 (2011). Accessed June 30, 2016. http://arxiv.org/pdf/1106.2443.pdf.

Goldberg, Elkhonon. "Gradiental Approach to Neocortical Functional Organization." *Journal of Clinical and Experimental Neuropsychology* 11:4 (1989), 489-517. Accessed May 14, 2016. http://elkhonongoldberg.com/images/gradiental%20approach%20to%20neocortical%20functional%20organization.pdf.

Grandin, Temple. "My Experiences with Visual Thinking Sensory Problems and Communication Difficulties." Autism Research Institute. Accessed May 19, 2016. https://www.autism.com/advocacy_grandin_visual%20thinking.

Grandin, Temple. "How does visual thinking work in the mind of a person with autism? A personal account." *Philosophical Transactions of the Royal Society* 364 (2009), 1437-1442. Accessed May 19, 2016. http://www.grandin.com/inc/visual.thinking.mind.autistic.person.html.

Hajer, Maarten A. *The Politics of Environmental Discourse.* Oxford: Oxford University Press, 1995.

Hayek, Friedrich. "The Use of Knowledge in Society." *The American Economic Review*, Vol. 35, No. 4 (September 1945). http://www.kysq.org/docs/Hayek_45.pdf.

Hernsoth, Nicole, "Exascale Timeline Pushed to 2023: What's Missing in Supercomputing?" *The Next Platform* (April 27, 2016). Accessed July 17, 2016. http://www.nextplatform.com/2016/04/27/exascale-timeline-pushed-2023-whats-missing-supercomputing/.

Hofstede, Geert. *Culture's Consequences, International Differences in Work-Related Values*. Newbury Park, CA: SAGE Publications, 1980.

Hossenfelder, Sabine. "Why Trust A Theory? Physicists And Philosophers Debate The Scientific Method." *Forbes* (December 10, 2015). Accessed July 24, 2016. http://www.forbes.com/sites/startswithabang/2015/12/10/why-trust-a-theory-physicists-and-philosophers-debate-the-scientific-method/#25e937763234.

ISO. "ISO in Brief." Accessed November 4, 2015. http://www.iso.org/iso/isoinbrief_2015.pdf.

Kains, M. G. *Five Acres and Independence, A Handbook for Small Farm Management*. Mineola, NY: Dover Publications, Inc., 1973.

Kriebel, David, Joel Tickner, Paul Epstein, John Lemons, Richard Levins, Edward L. Loechler, Margaret Quinn, Ruthann Rudel, Ted Schettler, and Michael Stoto. "The Precautionary Principle in Environmental Science." *Environmental Health Perspectives* 109:9 (September 2001). Accessed July 31, 2016. http://www.ncbi.nlm.nih.gov/pmc/articles/PMC1240435/pdf/ehp0109-000871.pdf.

Kuhn, Thomas S. *The Structure of Scientific Revolutions* (Chicago: University of Chicago Press, 1970).

Landau, Deb Miller. "Biometric Authentication – Is this the Death of the Password?" *iQ by Intel*, January 6, 2015. Accessed November 4, 2015. http://iq.intel.com/password/.

Leopold, Aldo. *A Sand County Almanac, With Essays on Conservation from Round River*. New York: The Random House Publishing Group, 1966.

Lieberman, Jeffrey A. *Shrinks, The Untold Story of Psychiatry* (London: Weidenfeld & Nicholson, 2015).

McDonald, Brandon. *Annotated List of Disciplines and Sub-Disciplines in the Biological Sciences*. Accessed June 19, 2016. http://www.cameron.edu/~bmcdonal/list/list/list.pdf.

McDonald, Brandon. "An Annotated List of Disciplines and Subdisciplines in the Biological Sciences." *Bioscience Education* 12:1 (2008), 1-3. Accessed June 23, 2016. www.bioscience.heacademy.ac.uk/journal/vol12/beej-12-c7.pdf.

McLuhan, Marshall. *Understanding Media: The Extensions of Man*. Cambridge: MIT Press, 1994.

Michaels, Patrick J. and Paul C. Knappenberger. "Climate Data vs. Climate Models." *Regulation* (Fall 2013), 32-6. http://www.cato.org/regulation/fall-2013.

Mokyr, Joel. *The Gifts of Athena, Historical Origins of the Knowledge Economy*. Princeton: Princeton University Press, 2002.

National Geographic 228:5, November 2015.

National Science Foundation. *Investing in America's Future: Strategic Plan FY 2006-2011*. September 2006. Accessed July 2, 2016. http://www.nsf.gov/pubs/2006/nsf0648/NSF-06-48.pdf.

Newport, Frank and Maura Strausberg. "Americans' Belief in Psychic and Paranormal Phenomena Is Up Over Last Decade." Gallup News Service, June 8, 2001. Accessed November 4, 2015. http://www.gallup.com/poll/4483/americans-belief-psychic-paranormal-phenomena-over-last-decade.aspx.

Novella, Steven. "The Increase in Autism Diagnoses: Two Hypotheses." Science-based Medicine. April 16, 2008. Accessed May 19, 2016.

https://www.sciencebasedmedicine.org/theincreaseinautismdiagnose stwohypotheses/.

OECD. OECD Family Database. Accessed October 7, 2015. www.oecd.org/social/family/database.htm.

Office of Policy Analysis, Smithsonian Institute. *Addressing Complexity: Fostering Collaboration and Interdisciplinary Science Research at the Smithsonian Volume I: Summary Study Report.* May 2009. Accessed July 1, 2016. https://www.si.edu/content/opanda/docs/Rpts2009/09.05.Complexit y.Final.pdf.

Pew Research Center Religion & Public Life. "Many Americans Mix Multiple Faiths." December 9, 2009. Accessed November 4, 2015. http://www.pewforum.org/2009/12/09/many-americans-mix-multiple-faiths/.

Pottage, Alain. "Too Much Ownership: Bio-prospecting in the Age of Synthetic Biology." *BioSocieties* 1 (2006). Accessed June 26, 2016. https://www.researchgate.net/publication/231845454_Too_Much_O wnership_Bio-Prospecting_in_the_Age_of_Synthetic_Biology.

Quandi. OECD Murder Rates. Accessed October 7, 2015. https://www.quandl.com/collections/society/oecd-murder-rates

Rainie, Lee, Joanna Brenner, and Kristen Purcell. "Photos and Videos as Social Currency Online." Pew Research Center, September 13, 2012. Accessed October 19, 2015. http://www.pewinternet.org/2012/09/13/photos-and-videos-as-social-currency-online/.

Palmer, Tim, "Build high-resolution global climate models," *Nature* 515:20 (November 20, 2014), accessed July 15, 2016, http://www.nature.com/news/climate-forecasting-build-high-resolution-global-climate-models-1.16351.

Porter, Michael. *The Competitive Advantage of Nations.* New York: The Free Press, 1990.

Power, William. *Hamlet's Blackberry, Building a Good Life in the Digital Age* (New York: HarperCollins 2010).

Rainee, Lee, Sara Kiesler, Ruogu Kang, and Mary Madden. "Anonymity, Privacy and Security Online." Pew Research Center, September 5, 2013. Accessed November 6, 2015. http://www.pewinternet.org/files/old-media//Files/Reports/2013/PIP_AnonymityOnline_090513.pdf .

Raymond, Eric S. *The Cathedral and the Bazaar* (2000). Accessed July 7, 2016. https://www.jus.uio.no/sisu/the_cathedral_and_the_bazaar.eric_s_raymond/landscape.b5.pdf.

Reardon, Jenny. "The 'persons' and 'genomics' of personal genomics," *Personalized Medicine* (2011) 8(1), 95–107.

Roy, Olivier. *Globalized Islam, The Search for a New Ummah.* New York: Columbia University Press, 2004.

Roy, Olivier. "The Transformation of the Arab World." *Journal of Democracy*, Volume 23, Number 3 (July 2012). http://www.journalofdemocracy.org/article/transformation-arab-world.

Rousseau, David, "The Software behind the Higgs Boson Discovery," *IEEE Software* (September/October 2012). Accessed July 12, 2016. http://indico.cern.ch/event/279648/sessions/143753/attachments/512195/706876/IEEE_2012_Higgs_Software_DavidRousseau_final.pdf .

Rzhetsky, Andrey, Steven C. Bagley, Kanix Wang, Christopher S. Lyttle, Edwin H. Cook Jr, Russ B. Altman, and Robert D. Gibbons. "Environmental and State-Level Regulatory Factors Affect the Incidence of Autism and Intellectual Disability." *PLOS Computational Biology* 10:3 (2014). http://dx.doi.org/10.1371/journal.pcbi.1003518.

Sacks, Oliver. "Inside the Executive Brain." *The New York Review of Books* (April 26, 2001). Accessed May 14, 2016.

http://www.nybooks.com/articles/2001/04/26/insidetheexecutivebrai
n.

Sacks, Oliver. "FaceBlind, Why Are Some of Us Terrible at
Recognizing Faces?" *The New Yorker* (August 30, 2010). Accessed
May 12, 2016.
http://www.newyorker.com/magazine/2010/08/30/face-blind.

Sarewitz, Daniel and Roger Pielke Jr. "Prediction in science and
policy." *Technology In Society* 21 (1999). Accessed July 15, 2016.
http://citeseerx.ist.psu.edu/viewdoc/download?doi=10.1.1.463.7525
&rep=rep1&type=pdf.

Schelling, Thomas C. *The Strategy of Conflict*. Cambridge, MA:
Harvard University, 1960.

Schumacher, E. E. *Small is Beautiful, Economics as if People
Mattered*. New York: Harper & Row, Publishers, Inc., 1973.

"Scientists Study Nomophobia—Fear of Being without a Mobile
Phone, A new questionnaire will allow research into a modern
phenomenon." *Scientific American* (October 27, 2015). Accessed
May 13, 2016. http://www.scientificamerican.com/article/scientists-
study-nomophobia-mdash-fear-of-being-without-a-mobile-phone/.

Shute, Joe. "Is it Time to Rethink Autism?" *The Telegraph*
(September 23, 2015). Accessed May 30, 2016.
http://www.telegraph.co.uk/news/health/news/11883482/Is-it-time-
to-re-think-autism.html.

Silberman, Steve. "The Geek Syndrome." *Wired* (December 1,
2001). Accessed May 23, 2016.
http://www.wired.com/2001/12/aspergers/.

Small, Gary W., Teena D. Moody, Prabha Siddarth, Susan Y.
Bookheimer. "Your Brain on Google: Patterns of Cerebral
Activation during Internet Searching." *American Journal of
Geriatric Psychiatry* 17:2 (February 2009). Accessed May 25,
2016.
https://www.psychologytoday.com/files/attachments/5230/136.pdf.

Steiner, Peter. "'On the Internet, nobody knows you're a dog' - New Yorker Cartoon." Condé Nast Collection. Accessed June 17, 2016. http://www.condenaststore.com/-sp/On-the-Internet-nobody-knows-you-re-a-dog-New-Yorker-Cartoon-Prints_i12265047_.htm,

Stodden, Victoria. *How Computational Science is Changing the Scientific Method.* July 29, 2009. Accessed June 20, 2016. https://web.stanford.edu/~vcs/talks/Science20July2009VictoriaStodden.pdf.

The Acarological Society of America. Accessed June 24, 2016. https://sites.google.com/site/acarologicalsociety/links-1.

"The Brain Technology Built: An Interview with Dr. Gary Small." *Neuronarrative* (December 15, 2008). Accessed May 25, 2016. https://neuronarrative.wordpress.com/2008/12/15/thebraintechnologybuiltaninterviewwithdrgarysmall/.

The Work of Edward Tufte and Graphics Press. Accessed November27, 2015. www.edwardtufte.com.

Tufte, Edward R. *The Cognitive Style of PowerPoint: Pitching Out Corrupts Within.* Cheshire, Connecticut: Graphics Press LLC, 2006 2nd edition.

United Nations Office on Drugs and Crime. *Comprehensive Study on Cybercrime.* New York: United Nations, Draft-February 2013. Accessed November 6, 2015. https://www.unodc.org/documents/organized-crime/UNODC_CCPCJ_EG.4_2013/CYBERCRIME_STUDY_210213.pdf.

Virtual Human Interaction Webpage, accessed at https://vhil.stanford.edu/ on March 24, 2017.
Wang, Shirley S. "How Autism Can Help You Land a Job." *The Wall Street Journal* (March 27, 2014). Accessed May 30, 2016. http://www.wsj.com/articles/SB10001424052702304418404579465561364868556.

Whitehouse, Andrew. "Do more children have autism now than before?" *The Conversation* (December 5, 2011). Accessed May 19,

2016.
http://theconversation.com/domorechildrenhaveautismnowthanbefor
e4497.

Winsberg, Eric. "A tale of two methods." *Synthese* 169 (2009).
Accessed June 20, 2016. http://www.winsberg.net/papers.html.

Winsberg, Eric, Bryce Huebner, and Rebecca Kukla.
"Accountability and values in radically collaborative research."
Studies in History and Philosophy of Science (2013). Accessed July
2, 2016. http://www.winsberg.net/papers.html.

www.ingramcontent.com/pod-product-compliance
Lightning Source LLC
Chambersburg PA
CBHW071430180526
45170CB00001B/289